maple

Library of Congress Cataloging in Publication Number:
2014953129

ISBN: 978-1-59474-804-2

Printed in China

Typeset in Futura and Scotch Modern
Designed by Sugar
Photography by Katie Webster, with the exception of
pages 1, 16, 70, and 100 (Kristy Dooley)
Production management by John J. McGurk

Quirk Books
215 Church St.
Philadelphia, PA 19106
quirkbooks.com
10 9 8 7 6 5 4 3 2 1

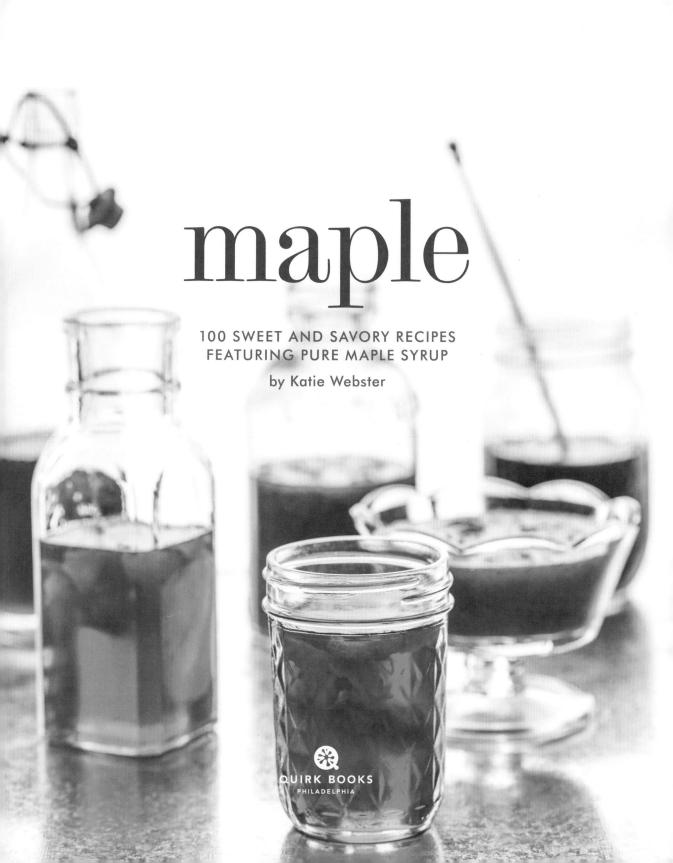

maple

100 SWEET AND SAVORY RECIPES FEATURING PURE MAPLE SYRUP

by Katie Webster

QUIRK BOOKS
PHILADELPHIA

Contents

Foreword

If I have learned anything in my thirty-plus years as a cook, food writer, and teacher, it's that the best tasting, healthiest ingredients travel from the farm, field, forest, or sea to our plates in the simplest, most direct way possible. It helps, too, if there's a good story to explain how these ingredients get to our kitchens. Indeed, I base much of my writing on the notion that eating becomes more meaningful—and tastier—when we know and care about where our food comes from.

Being a New Englander (and growing up with an uncle who had a maple syrup operation), one of my all-time favorite ingredient narratives is that of maple syrup. What could be more compelling than a sweetener that comes directly from our North American woods? That has been around since long before Europeans arrived? That is naturally sustainable and contains nothing but fresh maple sap boiled down to a delicious syrup?

You might say that a trickle of maple runs through my work. I wrote an essay on maple lore for my very first cookbook, and I have included maple in more than a few recipes, most of them savory. So I was delighted when I heard that Katie was writing an entire cookbook on pure maple syrup, and the more I learned about her approach, the more excited I became. Katie is the perfect author to take up the maple mantle. Although we live in neighboring towns and occasionally bump into each other at the grocery store, I know her more through her work as a recipe tester, blogger, and food stylist. Katie's energy and genuine enthusiasm for food, cooking, and life shine through on the pages of this book. She also brings to the project her invaluable DIY syrup-making experience, along with her passion for whole foods and devotion to a healthy lifestyle. The recipes reflect Katie's busy life as a working mom, but they aren't dumbed down. I've already put several into my regular rotation, and there are plenty more that I've flagged to try.

I believe that a good cookbook needs to be more than a collection of recipes; it needs to inspire and to teach. In these pages, Katie has achieved this goal, and she's done it with the same bright cheerfulness that accompanies her wherever she goes.

Molly Stevens

Molly Stevens's books *All about Roasting* and *All about Braising* won awards from the James Beard Foundation and the International Association of Culinary Professionals. She lives in Vermont and teaches cooking classes around the country.

Introduction

The composition is finally there. The fluffy pancakes are perfectly stacked. The lighting is just so. "Are you ready?" I ask the photographer. I get the go-ahead, hold my breath, and tilt the bottle. Golden liquid emerges, taking its time to ooze from the spout, and then the dripping begins. Soon it cascades from the top pancake over the edges to the lower layers, hesitating for a moment before making its way to the plate. The photographer clicks furiously, trying to capture the perfect trickle of glistening maple syrup. The light catches amber drops on the sides of the stack. We got the shot.

The image is instantly distilled into two dimensions. As a former food stylist—someone who cooks and arranges food for photographs—I know all too well how important this moment is. It's more than just a pretty picture: that flow and puddle of maple syrup mean something different to every person.

For me, the image evokes a snowy morning at my grandmother's house. Sausage frying in the skillet, and an enamel saucepan of syrup warming on the back burner. It reminds me of the evenings when the smell of steam rises on the quiet stillness of springtime air. The kids are tucked in bed, and my husband and I are boiling down the last of the sap late into the evening. It calls up the memory of the first time we took our daughter to the sugarhouse, the delight on her toddler face as she sipped the hot syrup from a tiny paper cup. It's the taste of Saturday mornings at our lake cottage: we're all in slippers and robes, my brother-in-law flipping blueberry pancakes and feeding everyone their seconds before he eats his firsts. It's staying ahead of the drips of a melting maple ice cream cone on a hot summer day.

Maybe to you, the same image recalls a lazy weekend morning spent with a newspaper and a cup of coffee. If you close your eyes, you can smell the unmistakable aroma that transports you to the breakfast table of your youth. Or for those who grew up in the North Country, you remember the delight of sugar on snow.

It is my hope that the recipes in *Maple* will conjure up and celebrate special moments for you. The foods you make may be new, but the sweet and aromatic flavors will surely be familiar. They will be nourishing, comforting, and above all delicious. Use them as inspiration. Each nibble, meal, drink, and dessert prepared with love is an opportunity to create new memories to cherish and treasure. ✲

How to Use This Book

When reviewing a recipe, if you come across unfamiliar ingredients or knife techniques, turn to pages 168–171. There you'll find helpful resources, explanations, and pantry notes.

The recipes in *Maple* are easily adapted to different diets. Throughout the book you'll see these symbols

which indicate that a recipe includes vegan, paleo-friendly, or gluten-free options—allowing you to quickly find dishes that fit your lifestyle. Note, however, that you should always double-check all ingredients you intend to use.

My goal is to provide recipes that are detailed and bulletproof, but I also want to encourage you to use your cook's intuition. Because equipment and ingredients are variable—heck, even the weather can affect a recipe!—it's important to be flexible. For example, I measure first by degree of doneness (e.g., "golden brown and bubbling") and then look at the timer. So, think of the time range as more of a guide to when the dish is likely to be done, with the visual as the deciding factor.

The Short Version of the Long History of Sugar Making

During the summer, maple trees produce starch and store it in their roots, trunks, and branches for the winter. Some of this starch is converted into sugar that, come spring, rises in the sap that then flows through the trunks. People have been tapping into that sap and boiling it down into syrup since before written history. Little has changed about the process, although the technology has evolved to improve the yield.

1700s Native Americans used maple syrup as a sweetener long before Europeans settled in North America. Lore suggests that they used syrup as a way to preserve maple sap, often boiling the sap until it turned into dry maple sugar, for longer keeping. It is unclear when European settlers first began sugaring or how they learned to do it, but by the 1700s iron and copper kettles were widely used by both Native Americans and colonial settlers to make maple sugar and syrup.

1800s Advancements in technology allowing people to bend tin arrived around the time of the American Civil War. With it came many improvements in maple production, from the invention of metal taps (called "spiles") and sap buckets to the development of more sophisticated boiling equipment (the precursor to today's channeled evaporator). With more control over boiling, sugar makers were able to process a larger volume of sap.

1950s The year 1959 saw the advent of flexible tubing for sap collection, coupled with vacuum pumps (an idea borrowed from dairy farming). Each bucket had to be manually pulled off the tree and emptied into a large collection tank on the sleigh while the sap was flowing. By contrast, the tubing can be set up before the run, saving a lot of time. It extends from tree to tree, and the sap flows from the tap into the tube and then downhill to a collection tank. The assistance of the vacuum pumps allow the process to be more efficient and extends the amount of time the sap can be collected. The combination of airtight tubing and vacuum pumps increases the natural pressure differential that causes sap to flow and doubles sap yields without hurting tree health. So, as long as you can walk to the trees, even those on steep slopes, you can tap.

1970s Reverse osmosis, first introduced in the 1970s, takes sap with a naturally occurring 2% sugar content and concentrates it to 12% to 15%. It can be done at the sugar bush (a large stand of maple trees used for sugaring), meaning that you will have to transport a much smaller volume of sap to the sugar house. You'll also have less water to boil off to concentrate the sugar content even further.

Backyard Sugaring

When I first moved to Vermont, I used to dread what Vermonters call "mud season." I couldn't understand why March weather was such a terrible combination of soggy soil, sticks, and cold. That first year I even took off my snow tires in March...and the next day it snowed eight inches! For years I just wanted the whole month to go away. Until, that is, my family discovered the joys of making maple syrup, or what my husband calls "backyard sugarin'."

I soon discovered just how fun early spring in the North Country can be. My husband, Jason, who had grown up in the state's Northeast Kingdom, was no stranger to the ins and outs of sugaring. He remembers gathering sap by horse-drawn sleigh as a boy. We started our family sugaring operation with only a few tools and some D.I.Y. equipment, plus my husband's knowledge from his childhood spent tapping trees.

All told, we tapped only five or so trees the first year. Then we had to figure out where to process the sap. After a few unsuccessful attempts at boiling it using our outdoor grill, and then hours of boiling indoors and steaming up the entire house, Jase decided to convert his parents' old wood stove for the task. He set up the 500-pound evaporator right in our driveway. Then he removed the top, where you normally load the wood, and fastened on an industrial hotel pan. Voilà! Once we started boiling, our neighbors began to appear as if by magic, driving up in their mud-spattered vehicles and looking to join in the fun.

Our first harvest produced only a few jars of syrup, all of which tasted mysteriously of hot dogs. (This probably has a lot to do with Jase insisting on showing the neighbors how good hot dogs boiled in sap can be, just as he remembered doing as a kid.) Thankfully, we've learned our lesson about a lot of things, hot-dog cookery included, and every year our production grows a little more. We start earlier, gather and prepare new equipment, and tap as soon as we think a whisper of a warming spell is in the air.

I still learn so much with each sugaring season. And every time I visit a real sugar house, I am reminded how makeshift our hobby is compared to the masterful skill used by the professionals. Though we're always improving, we're only a notch above the old wood-stove days. Jase dreams of building a sugar house somewhere on our property, but for now we still have our setup in the driveway. To me it doesn't matter—it's all about having fun. I've found that through the years, no matter what "system" we use, there are always a few constants: the mud, the cold, the warmth of the fire, the friends, the steam, and the sweet scent of syrup floating on the air. ✿

Tapping into Nature

Hobbyists can do their own sugaring with just a few pieces of equipment, though it also requires a commitment to the trees and a bit of instruction. Ideally, have someone with experience walk you through it your first time. Kits are available, and the websites on page 170 provide detailed information. Here's some of what you'll need to get started.

CLEANING SUPPLIES: Go online for maple-sugaring spiles and sap buckets or bags. Everything else can be found at the hardware store. Just make sure all your supplies are made of food-safe materials. Clean them well, avoiding substances that are toxic or will change the maple's flavor.

TREES: Sugar maples (*Acer saccharum*) are best, though any maple species can be tapped, including black (*A. nigrum*), red (*A. rubrum*), and silver (*A. saccharinum*). Make sure each tree is at least a foot in diameter. Change the location of your taps from year to year so that the tree stays healthy.

TAPPING: Use a regular drill and a $7/16$ or $5/16$ bit to drill a pilot hole in the tree (angled slightly upward is best, allowing gravity to help with sap flow). The hole should be 2 to 2½ inches deep. Tap in the spile, hang the bucket or bag, and then cover the bucket. At the end of the season, remove the splies with pliers.

THE RIGHT CONDITIONS: Sap flows when night temperatures fall below freezing and daytime highs are above freezing. The best runs happen when there's little or no wind and the tree's branches are wet with snow or rain. Once the temperatures remain consistently above freezing and the trees start to bud out, the sap can no longer be used—sugarmakers would describe its bitter chocolate and tootsie roll flavors as "buddy."

COLLECTION EQUIPMENT: Collect sap once a day or more often if the buckets are overflowing. Filter sap through cheesecloth or a felt sap filter into a large storage container, called a bulk tank, and store it below 38°F (3.3°C). Discard ice chunks that form in the sap buckets or bulk tank (it's mostly water, so you're not throwing away good sugar content).

BOILING EQUIPMENT: Fresh sap goes bad quickly, so boil it as soon as possible. Use a large, wide pan (such as a turkey-roasting pan) or low-sided pot fitted with a candy thermometer. Set the pan over a fire pit, or hang a pot over a fire. If you have a good fume hood in your kitchen, you can boil indoors. The object is to remove water from the sap to concentrate the sugar content. A rule of thumb is that 40 gallons of sap make 1 gallon of pure maple syrup. That's a lot of steam, so boil as much as you can outdoors. Once the sap has darkened and is considerably reduced but still thin, pour it into a small pan and finish indoors, where you can control the heat and keep a close eye on it. Stop boiling when the thermometer reaches 219.2°F (104°C), or exactly 7°F (3.9°C) above the boiling point of water at your altitude.

FILTER AND JARS: Filter the hot syrup through several layers of cheesecloth, a paper filter, or a fabric filter and pour it into clean jars. Use as soon as it is cool or store in the refrigerator for three to four months. Freeze syrup for up to a year.

Sugar Science

I spent a week in culinary school learning exclusively about sugar: sitting through hours of lectures, making candied sugar sculptures and confections, even spinning hot sugar into threads. So I've always felt like I had a fairly strong grasp of sugar science. But after testing and retesting the Salted Maple Penuche Fudge (page 160), I was thinking of renaming it something less flattering and throwing in the towel. After a week of unsuccessful attempts, I found myself at the farmers market, begging one of the maple candy vendors for help. She pointed me to Cornell University's Sugar Maple Research and Extension Program.

Fifteen minutes on the Cornell website and I'd realized that one week of culinary training was a drop in the galvanized-aluminum bucket of maple syrup science. After a lot more reading, several e-mails and phone calls, and many more batches of fudge, I finally achieved a more comprehensive understanding of the subject. The main thing I learned is what exactly makes candymaking with maple so unique: invert sugar.

A mixture of glucose and fructose, invert sugar is usually liquid and hygroscopic (meaning that it attracts and holds moisture), and it prevents sugar crystallization. It does that on a microscopic level by getting in the way of sucrose molecules as they cool, making the molecules slippery and unable to attach to one another.

Although all maple syrup contains some invert sugar, the level varies. Because of harmless microbial activity that occurs while sap is gathered and processed, the darker-grade syrup made at the end of the season (when the weather is warmer) has the highest level of invert sugar. Syrup made at the beginning of the season is lighter in grade and has a more consistent, lower level of invert sugar. (For more on grades, see the sidebar on the opposite page.)

When making fudge and candies, having just the right amount of invert sugar in the recipe is critical. I found that I had to start with the predictable amount of inverty syrup in Grade A Light maple syrup and then add a touch more in the form of corn syrup. I realize that to some of you this is absolute blasphemy. But as a true maple lover and maple syrup snob, I assure you that I had good reason. Although the dark syrup contains more invert syrup, it isn't enough to prevent crystallization. Adding a touch of corn syrup to these higher-temperature candy and confection recipes makes them set up correctly and consistently. You can also use golden cane syrup (found at good health food stores), which will do the same thing. But you'll need one or the other, because there isn't enough invert sugar in the maple syrup to prevent crystallization. 🍁

A Guide to Grades

If, when buying maple syrup in your local supermarket, you wondered about the grading system, you are not alone. The terms "Grade A" and "Grade B" have caused much confusion over the years.

Basically, the grades are a way to differentiate between the natural variations in the color and flavor profiles of syrup; they don't indicate quality. To help clarify the issue, in 2014 the state of Vermont adopted new grading standards, an effort joined by Maine and New York and which has spread to other states and Canada. It's likely that soon all commercially available maple syrup will be Grade A. (There's also Processing Grade, which is used in food manufacturing to provide the maple taste in products such as cereals, granola, turkey, ham, and sausage. It may contain some off flavors, and very little of it is available at the retail level.)

Below is a comparison of the old and new terminology:

In general, earlier-season syrup tends to be lighter in color and more delicate in taste, and later-season syrup tends to be darker in color and more robust in taste. That's partly because the sap gets warmer during the day later in the season, allowing more microbial action, which leads to a darker color.

But other factors can also affect color, including processing equipment. That happened to us. When we used to boil on our cast iron wood-burning stove, Jason rigged up a preheater made of a copper pipe with a coffee can attached to it. The pipe coiled down around the stovepipe, heating the sap as it drizzled down and emptied into the boiling pan. Unfortunately, the liquid would get so hot inside the pipe that the sap would scald, darkening all our syrup, early season or late.

old standard	new standard	taste
Grade A Light Amber	Grade A Golden	Delicate Taste
Grade A Medium Amber	Grade A Amber	Rich Taste
Grade A Dark Amber	Grade A Amber	Rich Taste
	Grade A Dark	Robust Taste
Grade B	Grade A Dark	Robust Taste

Why Choose Maple?

Even if you aren't tapping your own trees, there are plenty of good reasons to start cooking with maple!

It tastes good.
Part of what draws many of us to maple is its unique flavor, which comes from 300 naturally occurring flavor compounds. When you use maple, you're adding not just sweetness but a rich, deep caramel flavor that balances, mellows, and softens harsh flavors.

Because maple syrup is a natural, minimally processed product, it can vary by bottle, producer, year, and location. Its flavor and consistency are affected by the processing equipment and even local weather conditions. These factors make maple tasting a fuller experience than tasting refined sugars.

It's healthier than other sweeteners.
Unlike refined sugars, maple syrup has not been stripped of its micronutrients during production. It contains trace amounts of calcium, potassium, iron, phosphorus, and potassium, as well as more than fifty known antioxidants. With a score of 54, it falls lower on the glycemic index than many other sweeteners. It has anti-inflammatory properties as well.

Cup for cup, maple syrup is healthier than refined sweeteners, but it's still an added sugar. The American Heart Association recommends that women limit their consumption to two tablespoons of added sugars per day, and men should stop at three. The good news is that because you need less maple syrup than white sugar to sweeten a recipe, you'll save both calories and overall sugars when you make the switch.

It's better for the environment.
It sounds obvious, but one of the things that makes maple syrup unique is that it comes from a forest. It is not a cultivated product. Unlike granulated white sugar or corn syrup, maple is not made from a "field crop" that is planted and harvested in its entirety every year. Maple sugar makers use only a portion of what a tree has to offer. It is the sugar makers' reliance on the longevity of the forest that ensures good husbandry of the sugar bush. Buying maple sustains an unchanged wooded landscape and preserves natural ecosystems.

Furthermore, many smaller sugaring operations use wood, which is carbon neutral, to run their evaporators. And maple syrup itself is minimally processed without adding any chemicals. To make syrup, you are simply extracting water from sap to make a perishable product into one that can be bottled and stored.

It's better for small family-owned businesses.
Because of how maple syrup is produced, you can be sure that your purchase is supporting one or many small businesses. These smaller operations, many of which are family run, strengthen our rural communities and economies.

The large maple businesses that buy wholesale syrup from multiple small maple sugar houses and package it for retail are also directly supporting the smaller operations. As with all other ingredients we cook with, our intentional decision to know the sources of our food connects us to what we put on our tables. 🍁

The Flavor of Maple

It can be hard to describe the flavor of pure maple without using the word *maple*, but some other descriptors that come to mind are *caramel*, *wood*, *butter*, *nutty*, and *vanilla*. A chemical substance called sotolon mimics the flavor of real maple syrup and is used in artificial table syrups, maple extract, maple candies, and maple-flavored products. It can be found in spices and a variety of mushroom called a candy cap.

Of course, pure maple syrup's flavoring potential has its limits. Sometimes if I'm working on a recipe that I feel isn't sufficiently maple flavored, it's tempting to use extract to boost the flavor. I've also experimented with small doses of fenugreek powder (a maple-flavored spice common in Indian cuisine that is naturally high in sotolon). But every time I try either of these, the taste just seems fake or slightly off. Another temptation is to simply add more maple syrup, but doing so often makes the dish too sweet or pushes the amount of added sugar over the recommended daily limit.

The challenge when working with maple is letting the flavor shine through the other ingredients. Take it from me, a flavor hound who thinks more is always more: in some cases, assertive flavors like chocolate can mask the subtleties of maple. I find myself dialing back a bit on other flavors when I want to let the maple stand out. In a pie, for example, if you would usually go a little heavier on cinnamon, cutting it back will allow the maple to be the star.

Another way to boost maple flavor is by grade selection (see "A Guide to Grades," page 15). I find that going dark is the way to go. The recipes in this book use almost exclusively Grade A Dark, which has the most flavor and gives you the most maple essence. You can also pair maple with complementary ingredients that naturally bring out that elusive and indescribable maple essence and harmonize with it. I have come to think of these as maple's BFFs, and you'll see them in many of the recipes: bourbon, butter, celery (really!), dates, nuts, sherry vinegar, vanilla, coconut, rum, pork (especially bacon), anything that is smoked like paprika or chipotle, and did I mention bacon?

Maple also balances more pronounced ingredients, including vinegar, apples, and greens, as well as such Asian ingredients as miso, ginger, and soy sauce. I've also found that acidic ingredients like tart cherries, vinegar, citrus, and cranberries were my faithful allies in balancing the sweet side of maple. ☆

Sweet Substitutions

I have found a few helpful guidelines for using maple syrup in place of other sweeteners. These tips come from cookbooks like Vermont Maple Festival Blue Ribbon Recipes and the Cornell Sugar Maple Research and Extension Program, as well as through simple trial and error. If you'd like to try using maple in an old favorite recipe, just keep in mind that you will likely have to do a bit of tinkering to get it just right. Changing one variable often opens a can of worms elsewhere. But it's a fun challenge—and hopefully you'll come up with some winners.

A FEW POINTS TO KEEP IN MIND:

• If a recipe calls for 1 cup of white sugar, use ¾ cup of maple syrup. Particularly in baking, you'll also need to decrease the other liquids called for in the recipe by about 3 tablespoons per cup of syrup. Note, too, that maple syrup may cause baked goods to brown more quickly. Decreasing the oven temperature by 25°F will usually help prevent that from happening.

• Maple sugar can be used in place of granulated sugar without changing liquid levels, but remember that it is sweeter, so use slightly less, about ⅔ to ¾ cup of maple sugar for each cup of white sugar.

• If a recipe calls for honey or agave, substitute maple syrup one for one; start by experimenting with no other adjustments.

• Because maple is a liquid, and moisture activates gluten in flour, added liquid can give your baked goods unexpected texture. In these cases, it may be a better choice to use granulated maple sugar or simply avoid overmixing the batter.

• Maple syrup is hygroscopic (it attracts and holds moisture). Be careful cooking it to high temperatures as you would for candied nuts (page 58) or candied bacon (page 95). When substituting maple for granulated sugar in recipes like these, it will not stay hard and candylike at room temperature for long, especially if the weather is very humid.

Breakfasts

My husband's Grandpa Vernon, who lived and worked his whole life on the family dairy farm, started each morning by drinking a little dish of maple syrup. I always wondered why on earth he would do that. Wouldn't he want some pancakes to go with it? Or a warm bowl of oatmeal? Vernon was a notoriously no-frills kind of guy, and I fear this trait may be hereditary. My daughters would be just as happy as their great-grandfather to start the day this way. I'm not about to let them, but I have compromised just a little. Webster family house rule: the only time you can lick your plate clean is to get the maple syrup off it.

Easy Maple Turkey Breakfast Sausage

Finding good, local ground turkey is a lot easier than finding healthy turkey sausage. I like to know exactly what goes into my sausage, so I make it from scratch. If you want to cook only half at a time, you can freeze the rest raw.

Makes 4 2-patty servings | Active time: 15 minutes | Total time: 15 minutes

2 tablespoons maple sugar

2 teaspoons dried rubbed sage (not ground)

¾ teaspoon coarsely ground black pepper

½ teaspoon salt

½ teaspoon dried thyme

⅛ teaspoon ground nutmeg, preferably freshly ground

1 pound ground lean turkey

2 teaspoons avocado oil or organic canola oil

1. In a small dish, combine maple sugar, sage, pepper, salt, thyme, and nutmeg. Place turkey in a large bowl. Sprinkle spice mixture over meat and gently knead with clean hands, turning occasionally to incorporate spices evenly. Divide into 8 sections and shape into patties.

2. Heat oil in a large nonstick skillet over medium-high heat. Add patties and cook, turning once; adjust heat as necessary to prevent overbrowning. Cook 4 to 6 minutes per side, until browned on both sides and cooked through. Serve.

Potato and Sausage Breakfast Skillet with Greens

Although kale isn't yet considered standard breakfast fare, it pairs wonderfully with traditional morning flavors: skillet-browned potatoes, sausage, and syrup. This hearty breakfast is a contender for a new weekend brunch classic.

Makes 4 1-cup servings | Active time: 25 minutes | Total time: 25 minutes

1 large russet potato, diced

½ pound pork breakfast sausage, casings removed (if in links)

1 tablespoon extra-virgin olive oil

1 shallot, minced

½ teaspoon kosher salt

3 cups destemmed, finely chopped lacinato kale

2 tablespoons maple syrup

1 tablespoon apple cider vinegar

Freshly ground black pepper to taste

1. Bring several inches of water to boil in a large saucepan fitted with a steamer basket. Add potato to the basket and steam 5 to 7 minutes, until just tender when pierced with a fork or the tip of a paring knife. Set aside.

2. Meanwhile, brown sausage in a large nonstick skillet over medium heat, stirring with a wooden spoon and breaking up chunks, 3 to 4 minutes or until pink is no longer visible. Scrape sausage onto a plate and set aside; cover with foil to keep warm.

3. Add oil to the skillet and return heat to medium-high. Add shallot and salt and cook, stirring often, for 30 to 90 seconds or until fragrant. Add potatoes to shallots and cook, stirring occasionally, for 4 to 6 minutes or until potatoes are mostly browned.

4. Add sausage and any accumulated juices, kale, syrup, and vinegar and cook, stirring often, for 2 to 3 minutes or until the kale is wilted and just tender and sausage is heated though. Season with pepper. Serve warm.

Maple Chia Pudding Cups

The first time I tasted chia pudding, I immediately understood what all the hype was about. And you will, too! This is one of those versatile recipes that work year-round. I think of it as a blank canvas for flavors. Make it with whatever fruits or berries are in season, and add seasonings to suit your palate. Try skipping the vanilla bean and going with a bit of orange zest, or add a pinch of cardamom and top it with apples. Be creative!

Makes 2 1¼-cup servings | Active time: 15 minutes | Total time: 8 hours 15 minutes

Seeds of ½ vanilla bean

1 cup nonfat milk or unsweetened almond milk

¼ cup dark pure maple syrup

Pinch ground cinnamon, optional

¼ cup chia seeds

1 cup berries or freshly chopped fruit

V Vegan: Substitute unsweetened almond milk for nonfat milk.

P Paleo-friendly: Substitute unsweetened almond milk for nonfat milk.

1. Place vanilla bean seeds, milk, syrup, and cinnamon (if using) in a lidded quart jar. Close jar tightly and shake until liquid is well combined. If clumps remain, use a spoon to press vanilla seeds into the side of the jar to break them up. Add chia seeds and shake to combine.

2. Let mixture sit for 5 to 15 minutes, until seeds are softened and starting to gel. Shake well again. Refrigerate overnight.

3. To serve: stir to combine, divide into 2 bowls, and top with berries or fruit.

How to Split a Vanilla Bean

Use a sharp knife to split the bean in half lengthwise. With the dull side of the blade, scrape out the seeds. Don't discard the empty vanilla pods. You can use them to infuse liquor. Just place them in a jar and cover with vodka, rum, or bourbon.

Moo-light in Vermont Smoothie

I love to pour these creamy, dreamy milkshake-like smoothies into tall pilsner-style glasses. For the creamiest texture, use super-ripe pears.

Makes: 2 1¾-cup servings | Active time: 5 minutes | Total time: 5 minutes

1 banana, peeled and broken in half

1 very ripe pear, cored and cut into chunks

1 cup plain nonfat Greek yogurt

1 cup ice

½ cup nonfat milk

3 tablespoons pure maple syrup, preferably dark

1. Puree banana, pear, yogurt, ice, milk, and syrup in a blender on high speed for about 1 minute, until completely smooth.

2. Divide between 2 glasses and serve immediately.

Greek Yogurt Parfaits with Maple Vanilla Sour Cherries

Sour cherries are in season for only a short time, so pit and freeze as many as you can when you find them. My family does, and all winter long we pull cups of these ruby-colored gems out of the freezer. This cherry-vanilla sauce is special enough to brighten even the coldest, grumpiest of mornings. For an evening treat, add a splash of bourbon to the cherries when they come off the heat and spoon the sauce over vanilla frozen yogurt.

Makes 2 parfaits | Active time: 25 minutes | Total time: 1 hour 5 minutes

1 cup (5 ounces) pitted sour cherries*

3 tablespoons dark pure maple syrup

½ vanilla bean

2 cups plain, nonfat Greek yogurt

2 tablespoons flax seed meal, optional

You could use fresh or frozen and thawed cranberries instead.

1. Combine cherries and syrup in a small saucepan.

2. Cut vanilla bean in half lengthwise and scrape out seeds (see ingredient note, page 24). Add seeds and pod to the saucepan. Stir and bring to a simmer over medium-high heat.

3. Reduce heat to medium low and simmer, stirring occasionally, for 10 to 12 minutes, until the liquid thickens slightly.

4. Cool completely, about 45 minutes. Remove vanilla pod.

5. Layer cherry mixture, yogurt, and flax seed meal (if using) into 2 glasses and serve.

Snickerdoodle French Toast

This recipe is a mash-up of French toast and snickerdoodle cookies (a New England favorite). A quick flash on the hot griddle is all that's needed to melt the cinnamon sugar topping.

Makes 4 servings | Active time: 25 minutes | Total time: 25 minutes

4 large eggs

¾ cup low-fat milk

2 tablespoons maple sugar

¾ teaspoon ground cinnamon

4 teaspoons organic canola oil

8 slices hearty sandwich bread, whole grain if desired

⅓ cup maple syrup, warmed

1. Whisk eggs and milk in a shallow baking dish until combined. In a separate small bowl, stir together maple sugar and cinnamon.

2. Brush 2 teaspoons oil over griddle and heat to medium-high. (You can use a large heavy skillet instead of a griddle; just cook in 4 batches instead of 2.) Dip 4 slices bread into egg mixture and allow excess to drip off. Place bread in hot oil and cook for 3 to 5 minutes, until browned on the bottom. Flip and sprinkle with half the maple sugar mixture. Cook, adjusting heat to prevent the griddle from getting too hot, for another 2 to 4 minutes or until the bottom is browned. Flip toast onto the sugared side for 10 to 20 seconds to quickly melt the maple sugar mixture. If you need to prepare a second batch, keep warm in a 200°F oven.

3. Wipe griddle or skillet with a clean towel and repeat with remaining oil, bread, batter, and maple sugar mixture. Serve with warm maple syrup.

Overnight Whole Grain French Toast Bake with Dried Apricots and Chèvre

This recipe is perfect to pull out when you have a full house, as I always do during the winter holidays. The prep is done the night before, so just pop it in the oven when everyone rolls out of bed. For a hearty breakfast, serve this puffy golden casserole with a big fruit salad, steaming mugs of dark-roast coffee, and a pitcher of warm maple syrup (of course).

Makes 8 servings | Active time: 30 minutes | Total time: 10 hours

6 large eggs

2 egg whites

1¼ cup nonfat milk

2 tablespoons dark pure maple syrup, plus 1 cup for serving

2 teaspoons vanilla extract

1 teaspoon ground cinnamon

½ teaspoon freshly grated nutmeg or ground nutmeg

½ teaspoon almond extract

12 slices soft whole wheat sandwich bread, crusts removed

1 cup diced dried apricots

4 ounces crumbled fresh chèvre

½ cup sliced almonds

1. In a medium bowl, whisk eggs, egg whites, milk, 2 tablespoons syrup, vanilla extract, cinnamon, nutmeg, and almond extract. Coat a 9-by-13-inch baking dish with nonstick cooking spray.

2. Cut bread slices in half and shingle in two rows into the prepared baking dish. Trim bread to fit if necessary. Sprinkle apricots over the bread, nestling them between the slices. Pour egg mixture over bread, coating all slices. Cover with foil and refrigerate for 8 to 20 hours or overnight.

3. Preheat oven to 350°F. Bake casserole, covered, for 45 to 50 minutes, until the center starts to puff. Remove foil. Top with crumbled chèvre and sprinkle with almonds. Bake for another 20 minutes or so, until the top is golden brown.

4. Meanwhile, heat remaining 1 cup maple syrup in a microwave or small saucepan over low heat just until warm.

5. Let French toast sit for about 10 minutes before serving with warm syrup.

Maple Cranberry Walnut Granola

I love to make this treat for holiday gifts. It makes the whole house smell cozy while it bakes. Once it's cool, I just pack it into airtight jars and tie pretty ribbons around the lids.

Makes: 11 cups | Active time: 15 minutes | Total time: 2 hours

8 cups old-fashioned oats

1 cup dark pure maple syrup

1 cup walnuts, coarsely chopped

2 tablespoons avocado oil or organic canola oil

Pinch salt

1 cup dried cranberries

G **Gluten-free:** Use gluten-free old-fashioned oats.

1. Preheat oven to 325°F. Coat a large, rimmed baking sheet with nonstick cooking spray.

2. Stir oats, syrup, walnuts, oil, and salt in a large mixing bowl. Spread mixture onto prepared baking sheet. Transfer to the oven and bake for 45 minutes. Remove sheet from oven, stir mixture gently, and return to oven for another 10 minutes. Turn off oven but don't open the door. Let granola sit in warm oven for 20 to 25 minutes, until crisp and golden. Remove from oven.

3. Let cool on baking sheet. Stir in cranberries. Store in an airtight container at room temperature for up to 2 weeks.

Steel-Cut Oats Banana Walnut Bowls

Who knew something as humble and nourishing as steel-cut oats could seem so decadent? I love the way the crunchy coconut chips and walnuts play against the creamy banana and oats.

Makes 4 1-cup servings | Active time: 20 minutes | Total time: 45 minutes

3 cups water

1 cup steel-cut oats (Irish oatmeal)

Generous pinch salt

1 cup light coconut milk, stirred

¼ cup plus 4 teaspoons dark maple syrup, divided

2 bananas, sliced

¼ cup coconut chips, toasted (see page 167)

¼ cup chopped walnuts, toasted (see page 167)

G **Gluten-free:** Use gluten-free steel-cut oats.

1. Bring water to boil in a large heavy-bottomed saucepan over high heat. Add oats and salt and return to a simmer, uncovered, stirring often. Reduce heat to medium-low or low to maintain a gentle simmer. Cook undisturbed for 23 to 25 minutes, until water is absorbed.

2. Stir in coconut milk and ¼ cup syrup, increase heat to medium-high, and return to a simmer, stirring often. Reduce heat to medium-low and cook, stirring often, for 9 to 12 minutes, until oatmeal is still loose but no longer watery. It will continue to thicken as it cools.

3. Layer oats, bananas, coconut chips, and walnuts into 4 bowls, drizzle with remaining syrup, and serve.

Maple Sweet Potato Coffee Cake

When it comes to coffee cake, the topping usually steals the show. In this case, however, the moist, mapley sweet potato cake sure does even out the playing field!

Makes 1 12-inch coffee cake | Active time: 20 minutes | Total time: 1 hour 20 minutes

STREUSEL

½ cup chopped pecans, optional

½ cup all-purpose flour

¼ cup old-fashioned oats

2 tablespoons unsalted butter, melted

2 tablespoons dark pure maple syrup

½ teaspoon ground cinnamon

    Pinch salt

CAKE

1¼ cups white whole wheat flour

½ cup all-purpose flour

2 teaspoons baking powder

1 teaspoon ground cinnamon

½ teaspoon baking soda

½ teaspoon salt

½ teaspoon ground nutmeg

1 cup pureed cooked sweet potato*

1 cup dark pure maple syrup

2 eggs

4 tablespoons unsalted butter, melted

2 tablespoons avocado oil or organic canola oil

2 teaspoons vanilla extract

  * Steam 1½-inch cubes of peeled sweet potato for 17 to 21 minutes, until tender. Cool and puree in a food processor or mash until smooth.

1. Preheat oven to 350°F. Coat a 10-inch spring-form pan with nonstick cooking spray.

2. Make streusel topping: In a small bowl, use clean hands or the back of a spoon to stir pecans (if using), all-purpose flour, oats, melted butter, syrup, cinnamon, and salt, mixing until crumbly. Set aside.

3. Make cake: In a medium bowl, whisk flours, baking powder, cinnamon, baking soda, salt, and nutmeg.

4. With mixer on medium speed, beat sweet potato, syrup, eggs, melted butter, oil, and vanilla in a large bowl with until creamy and smooth. Add dry mixture to maple mixture and gently blend on slow until just combined. Spread in the prepared pan.

5. Top batter with streusel. Bake for 46 to 50 minutes, until the center is puffed and set. It will spring back when lightly touched, and a toothpick inserted in the center will come out with moist crumbs attached. Let cool for 20 minutes on a wire rack. Run a knife around the edges and remove sides of pan. Serve warm.

Maple Oat Zucchini Bread

These wholesome zucchini-packed loaves have a light maple sweetness. Slices are sturdy enough to pack into a lunchbox, thanks to a hearty dose of oats.

Makes 2 8-slice loaves | Active time: 20 minutes | Total time: 2 hours

2 cups white (preferably) whole wheat flour

1 cup plus 2 tablespoons all-purpose flour

2 teaspoons baking powder

1 teaspoon ground cinnamon

½ teaspoon baking soda

½ teaspoon salt

1¼ cups dark pure maple syrup

3 large eggs

½ cup avocado oil or organic canola oil

2 teaspoons vanilla extract

2 tablespoons butter, melted

1 pound zucchini, shredded
   (about 3½ cups)

¾ cup old-fashioned oats

2 tablespoons maple sugar, optional

1. Preheat oven to 350°F. Coat 2 1½-quart loaf pans with nonstick cooking spray.

2. In a medium bowl, whisk flours, baking powder, cinnamon, baking soda, and salt.

3. In a large bowl, with electric mixer on medium speed, beat syrup, eggs, oil, and vanilla until smooth. Beat in butter. Stir in zucchini. Add flour mixture and stir until just combined. Add oats and stir until just combined. Divide batter between prepared pans. Sprinkle with maple sugar (if using).

4. Bake for 50 to 56 minutes, or until bread is golden brown and puffed and a toothpick inserted in the center comes out with moist crumbs attached. Allow loaves to cool in pans for at least 15 minutes before turning out onto a wire rack to cool completely.

Maple Morning Glory Muffins

These are delicious warm from the oven, but they really shine as a make-ahead breakfast for mornings when you need to head out early. I make a batch on the weekend, and when the muffins are cool, I wrap them in plastic wrap and freeze in a resealable bag—they last for weeks. I let muffins defrost at room temperature or microwave them for a few seconds before I hit the ground running.

Makes 12 muffins | Active time: 20 minutes | Total time: 1 hour 30 minutes

1¼ cups gluten-free all-purpose flour

½ cup rolled oats, plus 2 tablespoons for garnish

2 teaspoons baking powder

2 teaspoons ground cinnamon

½ teaspoon salt

½ teaspoon baking soda

¼ teaspoon ground allspice

2 eggs

⅔ cup nonfat plain yogurt

⅔ cup dark pure maple syrup

¼ cup avocado oil or organic canola oil

2 teaspoons vanilla extract

2 cups peeled, shredded carrots

½ cup toasted nuts, such as walnuts

½ cup raisins

1. Preheat oven to 350°F. Coat a 12-cup muffin tray with nonstick cooking spray or line with cupcake liners.

2. In a medium bowl, whisk flour, ½ cup oats, baking powder, cinnamon, salt, baking soda, and allspice; set aside.

3. In a large bowl, whisk eggs, yogurt, syrup, oil, and vanilla. Stir dry ingredients into wet mixture. Then stir in carrots, nuts, and raisins.

4. Divide muffin batter among prepared tins. Sprinkle remaining 2 tablespoons oats over batter. Bake for 28 to 32 minutes, until muffins spring back when lightly touched and a toothpick inserted into the center comes out with only moist crumbs attached. Cool in the pan for about 10 minutes before transferring to a wire rack to cool completely.

Black Buckwheat Buttermilk Biscuits

I love the flavor of these lightly sweet black-hued biscuits. There are many methods for making biscuit dough, but I find that combining the butter and flour by hand or in a food processor yields the best texture with the least effort. Folding the dough a couple times helps create that lovely flaky rise that one associates with traditional buttermilk biscuits.

Makes 16 biscuits | Active time: 20 minutes | Total time: 40 minutes

2 cups all-purpose flour, plus more for dusting

1¼ cups buckwheat flour

1 tablespoon baking powder

½ teaspoon baking soda

½ teaspoon salt

10 tablespoons cold butter, cut into small pieces

⅔ cup buttermilk

½ cup dark maple syrup

1 egg, beaten

1. Preheat oven to 375°F. Line a baking sheet with parchment paper.

2. In a large bowl, whisk flours, baking powder, baking soda, and salt, or pulse in a food processor to combine.

3. Without overworking, cut butter into flour mixture until mixture resembles a coarse meal. If using a food processor, add butter and process a few seconds at a time until mixture reaches the right consistency. If using your hands, working quickly, rub together flour mixture and butter between fingertips and thumbs. If using a pastry cutter, press cutter to break up butter and cut mixture into small pieces.

4. Transfer mixture to a large bowl. Use a spoon to make a well in the center and pour buttermilk and syrup into the well. Gradually stir flour into the liquid center until dough comes together.

5. Place dough onto a lightly floured surface and press clumps together with lightly floured hands until it becomes a solid mass. Gently knead 2 to 3 times to make dough consistent but not tough. Pat out dough to a large rectangle about 8 by 9 inches. Fold dough into thirds, as you would fold to fit a letter into an envelope. Reflour the work surface. Use a rolling pin to roll dough to roughly 8 by 9 inches and ¾ inch thick. Fold again into thirds. Reflour and roll out dough again to the same size.

6. Use a 2½-inch biscuit cutter to cut out 12 biscuits. (Do not twist cutter.) Transfer biscuits to prepared baking sheet. Roll dough again and cut out 4 more biscuits.

7. Brush biscuit tops with egg. Bake for 13 to 15 minutes, until biscuits are puffed and lightly golden. Serve warm.

Cornmeal Waffles with Wild Blueberries

When I moved to Vermont, my first job was cooking in a bed-and-breakfast in Burlington. I woke up well before dawn to make breakfast for guests in the ten-room inn. Over the year that I cooked there, I loved to get experimental with waffle, pancake, and French toast recipes. Serving cornmeal waffles was a surefire way to surprise and delight the sleepy guests.

Makes 6 waffles | Active time: 20 minutes | Total time: 1 hour

1 cup nonfat buttermilk

¾ cup cornmeal

¼ cup dark pure maple syrup, plus ¼ to ½ cup warmed for serving

1 cup white whole wheat flour

2 teaspoons baking powder

½ teaspoon baking soda

3 large eggs, whites and yolks separated

2 tablespoons unsalted butter, melted, or melted coconut oil

1 cup wild blueberries, fresh or frozen (do not thaw)

Gluten-free: Use gluten-free all-purpose flour in place of the white whole wheat flour.

1. In a medium bowl, whisk buttermilk, cornmeal, and ¼ cup syrup. Set aside for about 30 minutes, or refrigerate mixture overnight, to allow cornmeal to soften.

2. Preheat waffle iron.

3. In a small bowl, whisk flour or baking mix, baking powder, and baking soda. Whisk egg yolks and butter into cornmeal mixture. Stir dry mixture into cornmeal mixture until combined.

4. In a medium bowl, use clean beaters to beat egg whites until soft peaks form. Fold into batter. Gently stir in blueberries.

5. Coat waffle iron with nonstick cooking spray or brush with oil. Cook batter according to manufacturer's instructions. Serve warm with remaining maple syrup.

Dutch Baby Pancake with Maple Rhubarb Compote

My mom never made Dutch baby pancakes when I was a kid, but my friend Christina's parents made them every time I spent the night at her house. We loved piling on the powdered sugar and maple syrup, which of course I recommend. Or, if rhubarb is in season, try this spicy tart compote spooned on top. You can make the compote up to three days ahead and store it in the refrigerator; just warm it in the microwave or over low heat on the stovetop before serving.

Makes 6 servings, plus 1¾ cups of compote | Active time: 20 minutes | Total time: 45 minutes

3 cups chopped rhubarb

½ cup dark pure maple syrup

½ teaspoon ground cardamom

½ teaspoon ground cinnamon

3 large eggs, room temperature

½ cup low-fat milk

1 teaspoon vanilla extract

¼ cup all-purpose flour

¼ cup white whole wheat flour

½ teaspoon salt

1 tablespoon avocado oil, organic canola oil, or coconut oil

1. Place a 9-inch cast iron skillet on the center rack of a cold oven. Preheat oven and skillet to 375°F.

2. Meanwhile, in a medium saucepan over medium-high heat, bring rhubarb, syrup, cardamom, and cinnamon to a simmer. Cover, reduce heat to medium-low, and simmer, stirring occasionally, for 10 to 12 minutes, until rhubarb is broken down. Reduce heat to low and keep warm until ready to serve with pancake.

3. In a large bowl, whisk eggs, milk, and vanilla. In a medium bowl, whisk flours and salt. Gradually add flour mixture to eggs, whisking constantly. Beat until completely smooth. Let rest for 15 minutes.

4. Pull out oven rack to access the skillet. Working quickly with a heatproof pastry brush, coat inside of skillet with oil. Pour batter into skillet. Push in rack gently to avoid sloshing batter onto the skillet sides.

5. Bake pancake for 17 to 22 minutes, until puffed and golden. Cut into wedges and serve with warm compote.

Lemon Poppy Seed Whole Grain Pancakes with Blueberry Maple Sauce

When it comes to pancakes, there are two camps: those who love fluffy style and those who love hearty whole grain style. These lemon poppy seed pancakes will make everyone happy. They boast an impressive rise, but they also have a satisfying denseness from the whole wheat flour. Whichever camp you fall into, the blueberry syrup is a must!

Makes 5 servings of 3 pancakes each, with about ½ cup of berries and sauce
Active time: 30 minutes | Total time: 30 minutes

3 cups fresh or frozen (and thawed) blueberries, divided

¼ cup maple syrup

2 cups white whole wheat flour or whole wheat flour

2 teaspoons baking powder

½ teaspoon baking soda

¼ teaspoon salt

2 large eggs

1¾ cups vanilla nonfat yogurt

1 tablespoon avocado oil or organic canola oil, plus 2 teaspoons for griddle

Zest from 1 lemon

1 tablespoon poppy seeds

1. In a medium saucepan over medium-high heat, bring 2 cups blueberries and syrup to a boil, stirring occasionally. Reduce heat to medium to maintain a lively simmer. Simmer, stirring occasionally, for 14 to 17 minutes, until blueberries break down and syrup thickens and reduces to about 1 cup. Cover to keep warm.

2. Meanwhile, sift flour, baking powder, baking soda, and salt into a medium bowl; set aside.

3. Preheat stovetop griddle to medium-high heat, or set an electric griddle to the pancake setting (400°F). While griddle heats, in a medium bowl, beat eggs until foamy and pale yellow. Beat in yogurt, 1 tablespoon oil, and zest. Stir flour mixture and poppy seeds into yogurt mixture until just combined.

4. Lightly brush griddle with ½ teaspoon oil. Ladle ¼-cup scoops of batter onto griddle surface; use the ladle underside to spread batter about ½ inch thick. Cook for 2 to 4 minutes, until bottoms are browned. Carefully flip pancakes and continue cooking for 2 to 3 minutes, until browned. If not serving immediately, transfer pancakes to a baking sheet or platter and keep warm in a 200°F oven while cooking remaining batter.

5. Serve pancakes topped with blueberry syrup and the remaining 1 cup whole blueberries.

Perfect Oatmeal Buttermilk Pancakes

This is the only recipe in this book that has no maple in it. But these pancakes are the perfect vehicle for the infused maple syrups on page 44. Or they're great with pure maple syrup on its own, of course!

Makes 12 pancakes | Active time: 20 minutes | Total time: 25 minutes

½ cup old-fashioned oats

1 cup all-purpose flour

¾ cup white whole wheat flour

1 tablespoon baking powder

½ teaspoon baking soda

¼ teaspoon salt

3 tablespoons cold unsalted butter, cut into chunks

2 cups nonfat buttermilk

1 egg, lightly beaten

2 teaspoons avocado oil or organic canola oil, divided

1. In a food processor with the steel blade attachment, grind oats for about 45 seconds, until the texture resembles coarse flour. Add flours, baking powder, baking soda, and salt and pulse to combine. Add butter and process until mixture resembles coarse meal.

2. Transfer oat mixture to a large bowl; use a spoon to make a well in the center. In a large measuring cup, whisk together buttermilk and egg until combined. Pour into the well and gradually stir until oat mixture is moistened.

3. Brush 1 teaspoon oil over the bottom of a nonstick skillet or 1 ½ teaspoons over a stovetop griddle. Heat to medium-high, when oil isn't smoking but a bead of water flicked onto the surface sizzles and evaporates in a second. Ladle ⅓-cup scoops of batter onto the griddle and spread them into circles. (The batter will be thick.)

4. Cook undisturbed for 2 to 3 minutes, until most of the bubbles that form have popped and the edges are starting to dry out. Use a spatula to flip pancakes; the bottoms should be browned. Continue cooking for another 1 to 2 minutes, until browned. Transfer to a platter or baking sheet to keep warm in a 200°F oven. Repeat steps with remaining batter, adjusting heat to medium-low to prevent scorching and rebrushing griddle with oil as necessary.

6 Flavorful Fruit- and Spice-Infused Maple Syrups

Think of these flavor combinations as a jumping-off point for your favorite seasonal ingredients and spices. A jar of infused syrup makes a fantastic gift from the kitchen (see page 166 for a sampling). Just be sure to keep them refrigerated.

BLUEBERRY MAPLE SYRUP

Makes ¾ cup | Active time: 10 minutes | Total time: 10 minutes

2 cups blueberries

¼ cup dark pure maple syrup

1. In a medium saucepan over medium-high heat, bring blueberries and syrup to a boil, stirring occasionally. Reduce heat to medium to maintain a lively simmer. Simmer, stirring occasionally, for 14 to 17 minutes, until blueberries break down and syrup thickens and reduces to about 1 cup.

LEMON MAPLE SYRUP

Makes ¾ cup | Active time: 10 minutes | Total time: 10 minutes

1 lemon (preferably organic)

1 cup maple syrup

1. Use a vegetable peeler to peel lemon into wide strips. In a small saucepan over medium-high heat, bring peels and syrup to a boil. Remove from heat and let cool to room temperature. Strain if using immediately. Or keep peels in syrup for a more robust lemon flavor; strain before using.

ORANGE NUTMEG MAPLE SYRUP

Makes 1 cup | Active time: 5 minutes | Total time: 5 minutes

1 orange (preferably organic)

1 cup maple syrup

½ teaspoon freshly grated nutmeg

1. Use a vegetable peeler to peel orange into wide strips. In a small saucepan over medium-high heat, bring peels, syrup, and nutmeg to boil. Whisk to combine and then remove from heat; cool to room temperature. Strain if using immediately. Or keep orange peels in syrup for a more robust orange flavor; strain before using.

CINNAMON MAPLE SYRUP

Makes 1 cup | Active time: 10 minutes | Total time: 10 minutes

1 cup maple syrup

1 teaspoon ground cinnamon

1. In a small saucepan over medium-high heat, bring syrup and cinnamon to boil. When mixture comes to a full boil, whisk to combine. Let cool to room temperature or serve warm.

CRANBERRY GINGER MAPLE SYRUP

Makes 1 scant cup | Active time: 5 minutes | Total time: 20 minutes

¾ cup fresh or frozen and thawed cranberries

¾ cup dark maple syrup

1 teaspoon finely grated peeled, fresh ginger

1. In a medium saucepan, bring cranberries, maple syrup, and ginger to boil. Simmer, stirring occasionally, for 14 to 17 minutes, until cranberries break down and syrup thickens and reduces to about 1 cup.

RASPBERRY AMARETTO MAPLE SYRUP

Makes 1¼ cups | Active time: 5 minutes | Total time: 5 minutes

½ cup dark pure maple syrup

2 tablespoons amaretto

1 cup fresh raspberries

1. In a small saucepan over medium-high heat, bring syrup to a boil. Remove from heat and stir in amaretto. Stir in raspberries and let cool. Mash berries with a potato masher or fork.

Drinks and Appetizers

One of my favorite chefs in culinary school explained that a meal should begin with a flavorful sip, to whet the appetite, and a highly seasoned nibble, to tickle the palate—not spill over the plate, overstuff the belly, and ruin what is to come. The following recipes are meant to do exactly that.

Maple Peach Old Fashioned

It's hard to improve upon a classic like the Old Fashioned, but this summery version, with muddled peach, maple syrup, and fresh cherry, may become a new classic in its own right.

Makes 1 serving | Active time: 5 minutes | Total time: 5 minutes

2 slices fresh ripe peach

1 fresh cherry, pitted

2 dashes angostura bitters

2 teaspoons dark maple syrup, or to taste

Ice

1½ ounces bourbon or rye whiskey

Place peach, cherry, and bitters in an Old Fashioned glass. Muddle with a cocktail muddler or wooden spoon. Add syrup and stir to coat fruit. Add ice, top with bourbon, and serve.

How to Muddle

Muddling is a technique used to release ingredients' flavors or natural oils A soft bruising is usually all that's needed; do not overwork. Gently press ingredients down and against the sides of the glass to crush the fruits and mix flavors. Muddlers are designed for comfortable and efficient work, but the back of a cooking spoon will do just fine.

Maple Meyer Lemon Whiskey Sour

I love the way the heady aroma of a Meyer lemon mixes flawlessly with the woody notes of bourbon. These whiskey sours are a welcome treat for chilly spring evenings by the fire.

Makes 2 12-ounce servings | Active time: 10 minutes | Total time: 10 minutes

½ cup bourbon

¼ teaspoon powdered egg whites, such as Deb El Just Whites

4 cups ice, divided

3 shakes angostura bitters

⅓ cup freshly squeezed Meyer lemon juice

¼ cup dark pure maple syrup, preferably dark amber

Pinch salt

2 lemon twists

* Run a channel knife around lemon rind, creating curly strips.

Whisk bourbon and egg whites in a cocktail shaker to dissolve the powder. Add 2 cups ice, bitters, lemon juice, syrup, and salt. Cover and shake vigorously about 45 seconds, until egg whites are completely dissolved and the shaker is cold. Divide remaining 2 cups of ice between two lowball or Old Fashioned glasses. Strain into the glasses. Garnish each with a lemon twist and serve.

Mapletini

This cocktail comes nowhere near a classic martini, and it's proud of it. It's best served arctic cold, so shake the vodka until your hands are stuck to the shaker by a layer of frost.

Makes 1 serving | Active time: 5 minutes | Total time: 5 minutes

3 cups ice, divided

1 (1-inch) slice of vanilla bean

¼ cup (2 ounces) good quality vodka

1 tablespoon dark pure maple syrup (or to taste)

1. Put 1 cup of ice in a martini glass and fill with cold water.

2. Cut vanilla bean in half lengthwise and scrape out seeds with the dull side of a knife. Add seeds and pod to a cocktail shaker. Add remaining 2 cups of ice, vodka, and syrup. Cover and shake until your hands are too cold to hold the shaker.

3. Pour ice water out of the glass, strain vodka mixture into the chilled glass, and serve.

Maple Margarita

Skip the orange liqueur here—the maple syrup adds plenty of natural sweetness—but add a touch of freshly grated orange zest. For an extra-frosty experience, chill the margarita glasses in the freezer before beginning. Just beware of brain freeze!

Makes 4 ¾-cup margaritas | Active time: 10 minutes | Total time: 10 minutes

4 lime wedges, slit across the center

Coarse salt for rims, optional

¾ cup gold tequila

½ cup freshly squeezed lime juice

¼ to ⅓ cup dark maple syrup

½ teaspoon orange zest

3 cups ice

1. Run a lime wedge around the edge of each glass and dip the rim into salt (if you'd like). Set aside. Perch a lime wedge on the edge of each glass.

2. In a blender, puree tequila, lime juice, syrup, and orange zest with the ice until no big chunks of ice remain. Pour into the glasses and serve.

Maple Sour Cherry Shirley Temples

My daughters light up with delight when I tell them that, yes, they can have a Shirley Temple when we go out. This maple-sweetened from-scratch version is so much better than the traditional overly sugared kind.

Makes 2 servings | Active time: 10 minutes | Total time: 10 minutes

1½ cups vanilla-flavored or plain seltzer water, divided

½ cup pitted fresh or frozen (and thawed) sour cherries, plus two for garnish

2 tablespoons pure maple syrup

¼ teaspoon almond extract

2 cups ice

Place ½ cup of the seltzer, cherries, syrup, and extract in a blender. Cover and puree about 1 minute, until cherries are pulverized. Strain through a fine-mesh sieve into a measuring cup or bowl. Fill two collins glasses with ice. Pour half of the cherry mixture over each glass of ice. Top off with the remaining seltzer, divided evenly between the glasses. Garnish with remaining cherries and serve.

Cinnamon Maple Punch

Here is a punch recipe I doubt you've come across. Taking the extra step of infusing the juice with cinnamon adds an unexpected twist on everybody's favorite party soft drink. Add slices of citrus and cranberries to the ice ring for a festive touch. If you expect a crowd, double it.

Makes about 7 cups | Active time: 10 minutes | Total time: 1 hour 10 minutes

2 cups apple cider

½ cup unsweetened tart cherry juice or unsweetened cranberry juice

2 teaspoons ground cinnamon

½ cup dark maple syrup

1 liter cherry seltzer

Slices of lemon and cinnamon sticks for garnish

Ice or ice ring

Over high heat, bring cider, juice, and cinnamon to a simmer, whisking occasionally. Remove from heat and let cool about 1 hour. Line a fine-mesh sieve with two layers of cheesecloth and set over a decorative bowl. Pour juice mixture through the cheesecloth. Whisk in syrup. Pour in seltzer. Add garnishes and ice or ice ring. Ladle into cups.

Sugaring Season Hot Cocoa

March and April on our hill mean sugaring parties and hours spent outdoors in cold temperatures. To warm up chilly little ones, I make a pot of this dark hot chocolate and keep it warming on the camping stove. Though the cocoa powder mostly masks the subtle maple flavors, we are flush with syrup at this time of year, so it wouldn't seem right to use anything but our own liquid gold to sweeten it up!

Makes 3 cups | Active time: 10 minutes | Total time: 10 minutes

⅓ cup best-quality cocoa powder

⅓ cup dark maple syrup

2½ cups low-fat milk

½ teaspoon vanilla extract

Marshmallows (optional)

In a medium bowl, whisk cocoa and syrup. Heat milk in a medium, heavy-bottomed saucepan over medium-low heat, stirring often, about 8 minutes, or until steaming. Pour hot milk into cocoa mixture, whisking constantly. Transfer cocoa mixture to the saucepan and return to medium-low heat, stirring often, until completely smooth and steaming hot. Stir in vanilla and drop in marshmallow (if desired) before serving.

Maple Switchel

This classic, refreshing drink was the great-grandfather of today's sports drinks. It goes down easy on a hot day or after a hard workout. For a drink that isn't as sweet, dilute it one to one with water.

Makes 2½ cups | Active time: 10 minutes | Total time: 10 minutes

3½ cups cold water

½ teaspoon grated, peeled fresh ginger

¼ cup unfiltered apple cider vinegar

¼ cup dark or pure maple syrup

Pinch salt

Combine water, ginger, vinegar, syrup, and salt in a quart jar. Cover and shake. Pour over ice to serve or refrigerate to chill.

The Best Tool for Grating Ginger

I love my rasp-style grater more than any other culinary tool. Okay, maybe that's an exaggeration, but I highly recommend it. The best-known brand is Microplane, but many other brands are good, too. Rasp-style graters are available in varying degrees of fineness and produce pieces that are much tinier than if using a box grater or mincing by hand. I use mine to grate ginger, garlic, and zest.

Pumpkin Maple Dip with Apple Wedges

I have been making this recipe for years. It's a favorite from when I was a personal chef, and I served it as a healthy after-school treat for the kids of one of my clients. Now that I have children of my own, I love to make it for informal neighborhood parties. Kids and grown-ups alike love to eat it with juicy apple wedges.

Makes 2½ cups | Active time: 10 minutes | Total time: 10 minutes

8 ounces reduced fat cream cheese or Neufchâtel

1 15-ounce can pumpkin puree

¼ cup dark pure maple syrup

½ teaspoon pumpkin pie spice

4 large apples, cut into wedges

In a large bowl with an electric mixer on medium-high speed, beat cream cheese until smooth. Gradually beat in pumpkin, syrup, and pumpkin pie spice. Continue beating until smooth. Serve with apple wedges.

Maple Spiced Pecans

This easy-peasy recipe is great to have on hand for surprise guests. The hardest part is letting the nuts cool before eating them!

Makes 3 cups | Active time: 5 minutes | Total time: 15 minutes

¼ cup dark pure maple syrup,
    room temperature

2 teaspoons unsalted butter, melted

2 cups pecans

1 teaspoon pumpkin pie spice

½ teaspoon salt

1. Preheat oven to 350°F. Line a rimmed baking sheet with parchment paper.

2. In a medium bowl, stir syrup and butter. Add pecans, spice, and salt and stir to coat. Spread nuts on the prepared baking sheet and bake for 8 to 10 minutes, until maple mixture is bubbling. Stir nuts to recoat with and continue baking for another 4 to 5 minutes, until nuts are sticky and thickened maple mixture sticks to nuts. Let cool before serving. Store in a sealed container in a cool, dry place for 2 to 3 days.

Note: If the weather is humid, the nuts may become tacky (See explanation on page 19).

Skewered Seared Duck with Tabasco Plum Sauce

When you combine the peppery kick of Tabasco, the sweetness of plum sauce, and tender strips of perfectly cooked duck, you have the makings of a culinary wow moment. The key to cooking duck breast is allowing the fat to render slowly, producing an unbelievably crispy skin and meat that stays medium rare. Serve with a chilled Gewürztraminer (or other slightly sweet, full-bodied white wine)—heaven!

Makes 24 skewers and ¾ cup of sauce | Active time: 25 minutes | Total time: 55 minutes

2 black or red plums, pits removed and cut into chunks

¼ cup dark pure maple syrup

1 tablespoon white vinegar

12 to 20 dashes Tabasco Sauce

1 whole star anise (or substitute ¼ teaspoon ground allspice)

1¼ teaspoons kosher salt, divided

1 pound (2 small or 1 large) boneless duck breast(s)

1. Prepare the sauce: In a small saucepan, combine plums, syrup, vinegar, Tabasco Sauce, star anise, and ¼ teaspoon salt. Bring to a simmer over medium-high heat, stirring often. Reduce heat to medium-low and continue simmering for 10 to 12 minutes, until syrup is thick and darkened and plums are soft and starting to break down. Remove star anise. Carefully transfer to a blender and puree, or use an immersion blender. Allow to cool. Sauce can be made up to 1 week ahead, covered, and stored in the refrigerator.

2. Preheat oven to 425°F.

3. Sprinkle remaining 1 teaspoon salt on both sides of duck breasts. Place breasts skin side down in an unheated medium cast iron pan or heavy-bottomed ovenproof skillet. Place over medium heat and cook, pouring off excess fat; if fat begins to smoke, reduce heat to medium low. Cook for 12 to 15 minutes, until fat has rendered and the bottom skin is crispy.

4. Flip duck breasts. Pour excess fat into a dish, set it aside to cool, and then discard. Transfer duck to the oven to finish cooking to medium rare, 4 to 6 minutes for two small breasts or 6 to 8 minutes for a large breast. Place duck on a cutting board and allow to rest for 8 to 10 minutes. Use a sharp carving knife to slice into thin strips. Thread strips onto brochettes or skewers and serve with dipping sauce.

Maple Pickled Ramps

Along with steam billowing from maple sugar houses, a sure sign of spring here in Vermont is the appearance of ramps, or wild leeks, sprouting along the riverbanks. Though their season is short, it is celebrated among old-time Vermonters and hipster locavores alike. Ramps preserve well when pickled, lasting for up to a month refrigerated in their brine. Use them in the Crispy Pita Rounds with Goat Cheese on page 62 or serve as a condiment on a cheese board with spiced nuts and charcuterie.

Makes 2 cups | Active time: 20 minutes | Total time: 1 day

⅔ cup champagne or white wine vinegar

¼ cup dark pure maple syrup

8 whole cloves

1 cinnamon stick

1 tablespoon kosher salt

1 tablespoon whole mustard seeds

¼ teaspoon red pepper flakes

2 cups (about 6 ounces) finely chopped ramps, root ends trimmed off

1. In a medium saucepan over high heat, bring vinegar, syrup, cloves, cinnamon stick, salt, mustard seeds, and red pepper flakes to a boil.

2. Place ramps in a clean pint jar. Pour boiling pickling solution over them and nestle the cinnamon stick into the jar. Seal the jar with lid and let it cool. Refrigerate for at least a day and up to a month before serving.

Crispy Pita Rounds with Goat Cheese

The sweet-and-sour pickled ramps have an unexpected, slightly bitter taste, but they pair seamlessly with the creamy fresh goat cheese in these little appetizers.

Makes 32 rounds | Active time: 20 minutes | Total time: 20 minutes

2 8-inch white or whole wheat pita rounds

4 ounces goat cheese

½ cup Maple Pickled Ramps, drained (page 61)

1. Place a rack in the center of the oven and another in the top position. Preheat oven to 350°F.

2. Use a biscuit or cookie cutter to cut each pita into 8 2-inch rounds. Pull apart the layers of each pita piece, for a total of 32. Place rounds on an ungreased baking sheet and bake on the center oven rack for 5 to 6 minutes, until crisp and toasted. Remove from oven.

3. Turn oven to broil. Top each toasted pita round with goat cheese. Broil on top oven rack, carefully monitoring and rotating as necessary, for 30 seconds to 3 minutes, until cheese is evenly softened. Top each with 1 teaspoon Maple Pickled Ramps and serve.

Brie with Maple, Walnuts, and Figs

This is a simple party appetizer, but one that you'll find yourself going to again and again. Although it requires little prep work, it looks oh so sophisticated. I like to wait until the last minute to drizzle the warm maple syrup so that it doesn't pool under the cheese. Serve with a variety of crackers and a sliced baguette.

Makes 16 servings | Active time: 10 minutes | Total time: 30 minutes

1 8-ounce wheel brie or other soft-ripened cow's milk cheese, cold

¼ cup chopped toasted walnuts

3 fresh figs, quartered

3 tablespoons dark pure maple syrup, warmed

1. Preheat oven to 375°F. Coat a small ovenproof plate or platter with nonstick cooking spray.

2. Cut rind off either the top or bottom of the brie and place the cheese, cut side up, on prepared plate. Press walnuts into exposed cheese. Arrange fig quarters decoratively over top.

3. Bake for 12 to 15 minutes, until warm and just starting to ooze around the edges. Remove from oven, let cool for about 5 minutes, drizzle with syrup, and serve.

Black Pepper Maple-Glazed Sausage Biscuit Bites

These canapés are lacking in pretention and bursting with flavor. They are a fun and unexpected appetizer to pass at a cocktail party, especially during the cooler months.

Makes 24 appetizers | Active time: 20 minutes | Total time: 45 minutes

- 1 cup white whole wheat flour, plus more for dusting
- 1 teaspoon baking powder
- ¼ teaspoon salt
- 4 tablespoons cold unsalted butter, cut into chunks
- ⅓ cup cold buttermilk
- ½ pound breakfast sausage, casings removed
- ¾ teaspoon cracked black pepper
- ¼ cup dark pure maple syrup, divided
- 2 tablespoons brown mustard
- 2 teaspoons chopped fresh sage, plus 2 to 3 sage sprigs for garnish, optional

1. Preheat oven to 350°F. Coat a baking sheet with nonstick cooking spray.

2. In a food processor, pulse flour, baking powder, and salt. Add butter and process until mixture resembles coarse meal. Pour in buttermilk and pulse until mixture just clumps together. Place dough onto lightly floured work surface and pat down until it is ¾ inch thick. Use a floured 1½-inch biscuit cutter to cut 12 rounds from the dough. (Do not twist the cutter.) Transfer biscuits to the baking sheet and bake for about 14 to 16 minutes, until puffed and browned. Set aside to cool.

3. Increase oven temperature to 425°F. Line a baking sheet with foil.

4. Form sausage into 24 small patties. Arrange on baking sheet. Sprinkle with pepper and drizzle with 2 tablespoons of syrup. Use a pastry brush to brush tops of patties, coating them evenly. Bake for about 9 to 11 minutes, until sausage is cooked through and syrup has caramelized slightly. Transfer sausage to a plate and cover with foil to keep warm.

5. Split biscuits in half horizontally and place on a work surface cut side up. Spread ¼ teaspoon mustard on each biscuit round and top each with a sausage patty. Transfer canapés to a serving platter, drizzle with remaining 2 tablespoons syrup, and sprinkle with chopped sage (if using). Garnish with sage sprigs and serve.

To make ahead: Bake the biscuits the day before and rewarm them before splitting them.

Maple Cashew Chicken Satay

Cashews are naturally a little sweeter than peanuts, so unlike peanut sauce, this cashew sauce doesn't need much sweetening up. I like to add a little lime juice to thin it out.

Makes 25 skewers | Active time: 30 minutes | Total time: 1 hour 45 minutes

2 small cloves garlic, minced or finely grated

½ cup cashew butter

⅓ cup lime juice

¼ cup dark pure maple syrup

¼ cup tablespoons reduced-sodium, wheat-free tamari or reduced-sodium soy sauce

1 teaspoon minced peeled, fresh ginger

¾ teaspoon salt

¼ teaspoon ground white pepper

1 pound boneless skinless chicken breasts, cut into 25 thin strips

Chopped roasted unsalted cashews for garnish

Chopped cilantro for garnish

 Paleo-friendly: Substitute 1 teaspoon Thai fish sauce for the tamari.

1. Soak 25 bamboo skewers in water for at least 20 minutes or up to 1 day in advance.

2. In a medium bowl, whisk garlic, butter, juice, syrup, tamari, ginger, salt, and pepper until completely smooth. Refrigerate ½ cup of the cashew mixture to use as dipping sauce. Add chicken to remaining cashew mixture, cover or transfer to a resealable bag, and marinate for 1 to 12 hours in the refrigerator.

3. Place a rack in the upper third and a rack in the lower third of the oven. Preheat oven to 400°F. Line two baking sheet with foil. Lightly coat foil with nonstick cooking spray. Remove dipping sauce from the refrigerator to serve it at room temperature.

4. Thread chicken onto skewers and arrange them on the prepared baking sheets. Discard marinade. Roast skewers, rotating pans once, for 12 to 14 minutes, until chicken is cooked through. Transfer to a platter and garnish with chopped cashews and cilantro. Stir dipping sauce before serving along-side chicken.

Soups, Side Dishes, and Salads

You'd be highly entertained to observe my food-obsessed family when we go out to a nice restaurant: our animated negotiations over who's ordering what, our exclamations of glee over one detail or another, our peppering the waitstaff with questions about unusual ingredients. Then we start to make deals with one another, ordering strategically so that we can sample as much as possible. My strategy is to choose the yummiest-sounding side dishes and most unusual salads and then consider the proteins to pair with them. And it's in that spirit that I approached these recipes.

Carrot Ginger Soup with Maple Yogurt

This soup is my personal health elixir. Anytime I feel the least bit under the weather, I turn to bowls of this gingery liquid, drizzled with creamy maple yogurt.

Makes 10 cups | Active time: 40 minutes | Total time: 1 hour

SOUP

- 2 tablespoons extra virgin olive oil
- 2 Granny Smith apples, peeled, cored, and chopped
- 1 large onion, diced
- 5 cups peeled, chopped carrots (about 2¼ pounds carrots)
- 3 stalks celery, chopped
- 2 tablespoons chopped peeled, fresh ginger
- 1½ teaspoons chopped fresh thyme leaves, plus more for sprinkling
- 1¼ teaspoons salt

  Freshly ground black pepper, to taste
- 6 cups vegetable broth
- 3 tablespoons apple cider vinegar, or to taste
- 2 tablespoons dark pure maple syrup, or to taste

MAPLE YOGURT

- ½ cup plain Greek yogurt
- ¼ cup dark pure maple syrup

1. In a large heavy-bottomed soup pot or Dutch oven, heat olive oil over medium-high heat. Add apples, onion, carrots, celery, ginger, thyme, salt, and pepper. Cover and cook, stirring often, for 15 to 17 minutes, until apples have broken down and vegetables are starting to brown.

2. Add broth, increase heat to high, and bring to a boil. Reduce heat to medium-low to maintain a simmer and cook, stirring occasionally, for 15 to 20 minutes, until vegetables are soft. Puree mixture with an immersion blender, or transfer in batches to a blender and puree. Stir in vinegar and syrup.

3. Make the maple yogurt: Whisk together yogurt and syrup. Drizzle on top of soup, sprinkle with additional thyme, and serve.

Slow Cooker Chicken Thigh Hot Pot

Traditional Chinese hot pots are cooked at the table, so this hearty slow-cooker stew technically doesn't count. Nevertheless, the flavors are inspired by a hot pot, and this countertop version is easy and delicious.

Makes 4 2-cup servings | Active time: 35 minutes | Total time: 5 hours

2 teaspoons avocado oil or organic canola oil

1½ pounds boneless skinless chicken thighs, fat trimmed

1 large Spanish onion, diced

1 cup sliced shiitake mushrooms

1 tablespoon minced garlic

1 teaspoon five-spice powder

½ teaspoon ground dried ginger

½ teaspoon crushed red pepper flakes, or to taste

½ cup dry sherry

4 cups low sodium chicken broth

¼ cup dark maple syrup

3 tablespoons reduced-sodium, wheat-free tamari or reduced-sodium soy sauce

2 tablespoons white vinegar

1 cup large-diced carrots

1 cup large-diced peeled celeriac

1 cup large chunks peeled yellow potato

2 tablespoons toasted sesame seeds

¼ cup thinly sliced scallions

 Gluten-free: Substitute wheat-free tamari for soy sauce.

1. Heat oil in a large heavy skillet over high heat. Add chicken thighs and cook for 7 to 8 minutes, until browned. Flip and brown other sides. Remove skillet from heat and transfer chicken to a large slow cooker.

2. Return the skillet to medium-high heat. Add onion, mushrooms, and garlic and cook, stirring often, 3 to 5 minutes, until onion is softened. Add five-spice powder, ginger, and red pepper flakes and cook, stirring, 30 to 90 seconds, until fragrant. Add sherry and cook, scraping up any browned bits, 30 to 90 seconds, until mixture comes to a boil and sherry is reduced by about one half.

3. Transfer onion mixture to the slow cooker. Add broth, syrup, tamari, and vinegar and stir to combine. Place carrots, celeriac, and potato on top (do not stir). Cover and cook for 4 hours on low. Garnish with sesame seeds and scallions and serve.

Smoky and Sweet Turkey Chili

The famed *New York Times* food writer Craig Claiborne once said that chili con carne, not apple pie, might be America's favorite dish. It certainly seems like it to me. My friends ask for chili recommendations more than any other recipe. So I knew this cookbook wouldn't be complete without a maple-spiked chili!

Makes 4 2-cup servings | Active time: 30 minutes | Total time: 40 minutes

2 tablespoons avocado oil or organic canola oil, divided

1 pound lean ground turkey

1 large Spanish onion, diced

1 tablespoon finely chopped garlic

½ teaspoon salt

3 tablespoons chili powder

2 tablespoons ground cumin

1 tablespoon smoked paprika

1 teaspoon ground dried chipotle, or to taste

4½ teaspoons red wine vinegar

1 cup water

1 28-ounce can crushed tomatoes, preferably fire roasted

1 15-ounce can dark red kidney beans, drained and rinsed

⅓ cup dark pure maple syrup

1 avocado, diced

¼ cup chopped cilantro

¼ cup toasted pepitas

1. Heat 1 tablespoon of the oil in a large heavy-bottomed soup pot or Dutch oven over high heat. Add turkey and cook, breaking up with a wooden spoon and stirring occasionally, until completely browned. Transfer turkey and any juices to a bowl and set aside.

2. Return pot to medium-high heat and add remaining 1 tablespoon oil. Add onion, garlic, and salt and cook, stirring often, for 6 to 10 minutes, until onion is soft and browned.

3. Add chili powder, cumin, paprika, and chipotle and cook, stirring, for 30 to 90 seconds, until spices are fragrant and starting to toast and darken slightly.

4. Add vinegar and stir for 30 seconds to 1 minute, until liquid is evaporated.

5. Add water and bring to a simmer, scraping up any browned bits and spices from the bottom of the pot.

6. Add tomatoes, beans, syrup, and browned turkey, stirring to combine. Increase heat to high and bring to a simmer. Reduce heat to medium-low to maintain a gentle simmer and cook, stirring occasionally, for 10 to 14 minutes, until turkey and onions are tender.

7. Serve topped with avocado, cilantro, and pepitas.

Sweet Potato and Peanut Soup

Sometimes when tinkering with a recipe, the stars align. This soup is one of those times. I first served it when all of our friends and neighbors came to help during sugaring season. We devoured bowlfuls drizzled with sriracha while standing around in our muddy driveway.

Makes 6 2-cup servings | Active time: 30 minutes | Total time: 45 minutes

1 tablespoon avocado oil or organic canola oil

4 cloves garlic, minced

3 cups diced onions (about 2 medium onions)

3 stalks celery, diced

6 cups vegetable broth

2 pounds sweet potatoes, peeled and cut into 1- to 2-inch chunks

1 teaspoon salt, or to taste

1 13-ounce can reduced-fat coconut milk

¾ cup unsalted roasted peanuts

¼ cup freshly squeezed lime juice, or to taste

2 tablespoons dark pure maple syrup

Chopped cilantro to taste, for garnish

Chopped peanuts to taste, for garnish

Sriracha to taste, for garnish

1. Heat oil in a large heavy-bottomed soup pot or Dutch oven over medium heat. Add garlic and onion and cook, stirring often, for 5 to 6 minutes, until onion starts to soften and brown. Add celery, broth, sweet potatoes, and salt. Increase heat to high, cover, and bring to a boil. Reduce heat to medium to maintain a simmer and cook, stirring occasionally, for about 15 minutes, until potatoes are soft and fall apart when pierced with a fork.

2. Puree soup with an immersion blender or carefully transfer it in three batches to a blender, puree, and return to the pot. In a blender, puree coconut milk and peanuts for about 1 minute, until completely smooth, scraping down the sides as necessary. Stir coconut mixture, lime juice, and syrup into the soup. Gently stir over low heat to warm through; do not boil. Serve garnished with cilantro, chopped peanuts, and sriracha.

Sweet Potato Casserole with Maple Pecans and Italian Meringue

Having a side dish that doesn't spend much time in the oven is something to be thankful for, so here's a mapley spin on a Thanksgiving classic. To make the meringue, I use the maple syrup just as you would sugar syrup, and it works like a charm.

Makes 16 ⅔-cup serving | Active time: 40 minutes | Total time: 50 minutes

4 pounds sweet potatoes, peeled and cut into 1½-inch chunks

4 tablespoons unsalted butter, divided

1½ teaspoon salt, plus a pinch, divided

¼ teaspoon ground cinnamon

Pinch ground dried chipotle

1 cup orange juice, preferably freshly squeezed

2 large egg whites, room temperature*

⅓ cup plus 1 tablespoon dark pure maple syrup, divided

½ cup chopped pecans

To warm egg whites to room temperature quickly and safely, place whole eggs in a small bowl. Cover with very warm water and let sit several minutes. Drain and separate eggs as usual.

1. Place sweet potatoes in a large saucepan and cover generously with cold water. Bring to a boil over high heat. Reduce heat to simmer and cook for 15 to 20 minutes, until potatoes are tender when pierced with a fork. Drain and return potatoes to the pot. Add 3 tablespoons of the butter, 1¼ teaspoons of the salt, cinnamon, and chipotle. Mash potatoes until no large lumps remain. Add orange juice and stir. Cover to keep warm.

2. Place a rack in the upper third of the oven. Heat broiler. Coat a broiler-safe 2½-quart casserole dish with cooking spray.

3. In a stand mixer with a whisk attachment, beat egg whites and ¼ teaspoon salt at medium-high speed until soft peaks form. Meanwhile, in a small saucepan over medium-high heat, bring ⅓ cup of the syrup to a simmer. Boil undisturbed until a candy thermometer reaches 238°F. With the mixer beating continually on high, immediately drizzle hot syrup into egg white mixture. Continue beating for another 2 minutes, until the bottom of the mixing bowl is only slightly warm. Scoop meringue into a large resealable bag and set aside.

4. In a small saucepan over medium heat, mix remaining 1 tablespoon syrup, 1 tablespoon butter, and pinch of salt. Bring to a boil. Add pecans and cook, stirring constantly, for 1 to 2 minutes, until nuts are coated.

5. Spread sweet potato mixture into the casserole dish. Top with pecans. Cut the corner off the resealable bag and pipe meringue decoratively over sweet potato mixture. Broil, rotating as necessary, for 30 seconds to 2 minutes, until top is browned. Serve.

Maple Glazed Carrots

What would a maple syrup cookbook be without a classic glazed carrot recipe? This one has the requisite butter, but only a touch.

Makes 4 cups | Active time: 25 minutes | Total time: 25 minutes

1 tablespoon unsalted butter

1 shallot, minced

¼ cup water

¼ cup dark pure maple syrup

½ teaspoon salt, or to taste

¼ teaspoon ground cinnamon

5 cups sliced carrots, about ¼-inch thick

4 teaspoons apple cider vinegar

1. Heat butter in a large heavy skillet over medium-high heat. Add shallot and cook, stirring, 1 to 2 minutes, until soft and browned. Add water, syrup, salt, and cinnamon. Increase heat to high and bring to a boil, stirring occasionally. Add carrots and return to a simmer, stirring occasionally.

2. Cover, reduce heat to medium to maintain a lively simmer, and cook, stirring once or twice, 4 to 6 minutes, until carrots are crisp-tender. Remove lid and stir in vinegar. Increase heat to medium-high and continue cooking, stirring often, 3 to 5 minutes, until liquid has thickened and carrots are coated. Serve warm.

Sap Baked Beans

Don't worry, you can make these extra-saucy, sweet, and smoky baked beans even when the sap isn't running. Just simmer the beans in a mixture of water and maple syrup, instead of sap.

Makes 9½ cups | Active time: 20 minutes | Total time: 12 hours

1 pound dry yellow eye beans, rinsed and cleaned of debris

4 cups water

4 slices raw bacon, diced

1 tablespoon avocado oil or organic canola oil

2 cups diced onion

2 cloves garlic, minced

4 cups fresh maple sap, filtered or strained*

¼ cup maple syrup

1½ teaspoons smoked paprika

1 28-ounce can peeled whole tomatoes, drained and crushed by hand

2 tablespoons apple cider vinegar

1 tablespoon Dijon mustard

1 teaspoon salt

If you don't have fresh maple sap, use 4 cups water mixed with 2 tablespoons dark pure maple syrup.

1. Combine beans and water in a bowl and let soak overnight.

2. Place bacon in a large heavy-bottomed Dutch oven over medium heat. Cook, stirring often, 8 to 14 minutes, until bacon is crispy. Remove from heat. Spoon bacon pieces onto a towel-lined plate. Pour off bacon fat and discard.

3. Preheat oven to 325°F.

4. Add oil to the Dutch oven and place over medium-high heat. Add onion and garlic and cook, stirring often, 5 to 6 minutes, until onion is softened and starting to brown. Add sap, syrup, and paprika and bring to a boil. Drain beans and add to boiling sap. Return to a simmer. Cover and transfer to the oven.

5. Bake beans about 1 hour, until almost tender but not split. Stir in tomatoes, vinegar, mustard, and salt. Cover and return to the oven. Bake for about 1 hour, until beans are completely tender and sauce is thickened. Stir in cooked bacon and serve.

Kale Skillet Salad with Walnuts and Maple

How is this kale salad like a martini? It's all about getting the sublime balance of tastes. In the case of this warm sweet salad it's a blend of sour, bitter, and salty.

Makes 4 ¾-cup servings | Active time: 20 minutes | Total time: 20 minutes

4½ teaspoons malt vinegar

2 tablespoons dark maple syrup, divided

1 tablespoon coarse mustard

½ teaspoon salt

Freshly ground black pepper, to taste

2 tablespoons extra-virgin olive oil

1 large shallot, sliced

10 cups thinly sliced, destemmed kale (about ½ pound)

¼ cup chopped toasted walnuts

1. Stir vinegar, 1 tablespoon syrup, mustard, salt, and pepper in a small bowl. Set aside.

2. Heat oil in a large heavy skillet over medium-high heat. Add shallot and cook, stirring constantly, 1 to 3 minutes, until soft and browned. Add kale and vinegar mixture and stir to coat, 30 seconds to 2 minutes, until kale is bright green and just starting to wilt. Remove from heat and season with pepper.

3. Serve kale sprinkled with walnuts and drizzled with remaining 1 tablespoon syrup.

Sweet and Sour Skillet Sauerkraut

This quick sauerkraut has classic flavors plus natural sweetness from caramelized onion and pure maple syrup. For a fancier dish, serve with the Maple Pork Loin Roast with Apple Chutney (page 120). Or for a more casual meal, pair it with mild German-style sausages such as bockwurst or bratwurst or tuck it into a reuben sandwich.

Makes 2½ cups | Active time: 20 minutes | Total time: 20 minutes

1 tablespoon avocado oil or organic canola oil

1 small sweet onion, thinly sliced

4 cups finely sliced cabbage (chop horizontally if strips are long)

2 to 4 tablespoons water

2 tablespoons white vinegar

¾ teaspoon salt

½ teaspoon caraway seeds

4 teaspoons dark pure maple syrup

1. Swirl oil in the bottom of a large heavy skillet. Add onion and place over medium heat. Cook, stirring often, 4 to 6 minutes, until onions are softened slightly and just starting to brown.

2. Add cabbage, 2 tablespoons water, vinegar, salt, and caraway and increase heat to medium high. Cook, stirring occasionally, adding up to 2 more tablespoons water if needed to prevent cabbage from browning, 5 to 8 minutes, until cabbage is wilted and crisp tender. Remove from heat and drizzle with syrup. Toss to coat and serve.

Layered Beet and Carrot Salad

This brightly colored and flavored root vegetable slaw is festive at a holiday meal. Layered in a glass dish, it almost resembles a trifle.

Makes 12 ¾-cup servings | Active time: 1 hour | Total time: 1 hour

5 carrots, peeled and shredded (about 2½ cups)

4 large beets, peeled and shredded (about 5 cups)

1 small shallot, minced

¼ cup apple cider vinegar

2 tablespoon extra-virgin olive oil

3 tablespoons dark pure maple syrup

1½ teaspoons Dijon mustard

¾ teaspoon salt

¼ teaspoon freshly ground black pepper

4 strips cooked bacon, crumbled

1 cup shredded sharp cheddar cheese

½ cup roughly chopped Maple Spiced Pecans (page 58) or toasted pecans

1. Place carrots in one medium bowl and beets in another. In a small dish, whisk shallot, vinegar, oil, syrup, mustard, salt, and pepper. Drizzle over carrots and beets, dividing evenly between both. Toss to coat.

2. In a large glass bowl, alternate two layers each of beets, carrots, bacon, cheddar, and pecans. Serve drizzled with leftover dressing from beets and carrots.

Sweet and Sour Coleslaw

I brought this dish to a friend's annual fried chicken dinner, and everyone agreed that the sweet and tangy salad was the perfect crunchy foil for the main entree. Feel free to double the recipe if you're serving a big crowd—the leftovers, if there are any, are delicious.

Makes 8 cups | Active time: 15 minutes | Total time: 15 minutes

3 tablespoons white vinegar or apple cider vinegar

2 tablespoons dark pure maple syrup

1 tablespoon flax seed oil

2 teaspoons avocado oil or organic canola oil

½ teaspoon salt

¼ teaspoon freshly ground black pepper

1 small apple, julienned

8 cups finely chopped cabbage

½ cup finely diced carrots

Whisk vinegar, syrup, oils, salt, and pepper in a large bowl. Add apple, cabbage, and carrots and toss to coat. Serve.

How to Use Flax Seed Oil

Flax seed oil is found in the refrigerated section of health food stores and large supermarkets. It is heat sensitive, so don't cook with it; store it in the refrigerator. Its slightly nutty, almost fishy flavor is best when paired with bold flavors.

Sherry Orange Quinoa

I love the way the woodsy notes in the sherry vinegar highlight the maple in this dressing. Serve the quinoa warm or at room temperature.

Makes 8 servings (each 1 cup of quinoa and 1 cup of arugula) | Active time: 25 minutes | Total time: 30 minutes

6 strips uncooked bacon, chopped

¼ cup extra-virgin olive oil, divided

1 red onion, diced

4 cups water

2 cups rinsed quinoa

¾ teaspoon salt

¼ cup dark pure maple syrup

2 tablespoons sherry vinegar

1 teaspoon Dijon mustard

1 teaspoon orange zest

½ teaspoon freshly ground black pepper

1 cup chopped curly-leaf parsley

8 cups baby arugula

1. Place bacon in a large saucepan. Cook over medium heat, stirring often, 7 to 10 minutes, until crispy and browned. Transfer to a paper-towel-lined plate and pour off fat from saucepan.

2. To the saucepan, add 1 tablespoon oil and onion. Return to medium-high heat and cook, stirring often, 4 to 6 minutes, until onion is softened and starting to brown. Add water, quinoa, and salt, increase heat to high, and bring to a simmer, stirring occasionally. Cover and reduce heat to medium-low or low to maintain a simmer. Simmer for 18 to 22 minutes, until water is absorbed and quinoa is tender.

3. Meanwhile, in a large bowl, whisk syrup, vinegar, mustard, zest, pepper, and the remaining 3 tablespoons oil.

4. Add hot quinoa and stir to coat. Stir in parsley and bacon. Mound on top of arugula to serve.

German Potato Salad

Want to change up your usual potato salad? Ditch the mayo and opt for an oil-and-vinegar dressing instead. The smoked paprika boosts the flavor of the bacon and adds a reddish tint to this maple-spiked warm weather classic.

Makes 7 cups | Active time: 25 minutes | Total time: 1 hour 20 minutes

2 pounds small thin-skinned potatoes, cut into 1-inch pieces

¼ cup extra virgin olive oil

¼ cup apple cider vinegar

3 tablespoons dark pure maple syrup

1 teaspoon salt

½ teaspoon freshly ground black pepper, or to taste

½ teaspoon smoked paprika

5 strips bacon, cooked and crumbled

1 cup finely chopped celery, preferably with leaves

½ cup minced red onion

½ cup chopped parsley

1. In a saucepan fitted with a steamer basket, bring several inches of water to boil over high heat. Add potatoes, cover, and cook for 17 to 21 minutes, until potatoes are tender when pierced with a fork.

2. Meanwhile, in a large bowl, whisk oil, vinegar, syrup, salt, pepper, and paprika.

3. Add hot potatoes to dressing and toss to coat. Cool, stirring once or twice, 15 to 45 minutes, until just warm or at room temperature. Add bacon, celery, onion, and parsley and stir to combine. Serve at room temperature or refrigerate until ready to serve.

Black-Eyed Pea Salad with Roasted Peppers

I grew up eating a variation of this black-eyed pea salad known as Texas Caviar. Our family recipe calls for store-bought Italian dressing. These days I prefer to make my own, giving it a fiery kick from ground chipotle and a little sweetness from pure maple syrup.

Makes 7 cups | Active time: 40 minutes | Total time: 10 hours

2 cups dry black-eyed peas, rinsed and cleaned of debris

2 bell peppers

1 clove garlic, minced

2 teaspoons kosher salt, divided

½ cup extra virgin olive oil

⅓ cup red wine vinegar

3 tablespoons dark pure maple syrup

½ teaspoon freshly ground black pepper

¼ teaspoon ground dried chipotle, or to taste

2 jalapeños, minced, seeds included to taste

1 bunch scallions, thinly sliced

1. Soak black-eyed peas in a large bowl of water overnight, or for at least 7 hours. Drain and place in a large saucepan. Cover with a generous amount of water and bring to a boil over high heat. Reduce heat to maintain a gentle simmer and cook for about 20 minutes, until tender.

2. Meanwhile, place a rack in the upper third of the oven and turn on broiler. Line a heavy baking sheet with aluminum foil and place bell peppers on it. Broil peppers, turning with tongs every 3 to 5 minutes, for 15 to 20 minutes total, until skin is blackened and blistered. Transfer peppers to a heatproof bowl, cover with foil, and let rest for about 20 minutes, until cool enough to handle. Peel off blackened skin and remove seeds. Dice flesh and set aside.

3. Sprinkle 1 teaspoon salt over garlic and mash with the side of a chef's knife to form a paste. Transfer garlic paste to a large bowl. Whisk in remaining 1 teaspoon salt, olive oil, vinegar, syrup, black pepper, and chipotle.

4. When peas are tender, drain thoroughly and add to dressing. Stir in jalapeños and diced roasted peppers. Refrigerate for up to 2 days. Stir in scallions before serving.

Cauliflower Salad with Black Sesame

As Mary Poppins wisely said, "Just a spoonful of sugar helps the medicine go down." In our house, a spoonful of maple syrup helps the cauliflower go down. My children love this recipe and always ask for seconds. Who knew cauliflower could be so kid friendly?

Makes 4 cups | Active time: 10 minutes | Total time: 10 minutes   Ⓖ Ⓥ

2 tablespoons dark pure maple syrup

2 teaspoons Dijon mustard

2 tablespoons reduced-sodium soy sauce or reduced-sodium, wheat-free tamari

1 tablespoon toasted sesame oil

2 teaspoons white vinegar

4 cups cauliflower pieces (about ½ head)

½ cup sliced scallions (about ½ bunch)

2 teaspoons black and/or white sesame seeds

Ⓖ **Gluten-free:** Substitute wheat-free tamari for soy sauce.

In a large bowl, whisk syrup and mustard until smooth. Whisk in soy sauce, sesame oil, and vinegar. Add cauliflower, scallions, and sesame seeds. Toss until completely coated and serve.

Spinach Salad with Blue Cheese and Candied Bacon

If it's possible for a salad to change your life, then this is that salad.

Makes 4 entrée-sized servings or 8 side salads | Active time: 25 minutes | Total time: 1 hour

8 strips bacon

¼ cup dark pure maple syrup

¼ teaspoon coarsely ground black pepper

14 cups baby spinach

1 cup sliced radishes

½ cup salad dressing, such as Maple Balsamic Vinaigrette (page 96)

½ cup crumbled blue cheese

2 tablespoons chopped chives

1. Preheat oven to 400°F. Line a baking sheet with parchment paper or a silicone baking liner.

2. Lay bacon on the baking sheet. Bake for 14 to 20 minutes, until bacon is crispy and fat has rendered. Remove from the oven and carefully pour off as much fat as possible. Pour syrup over bacon and sprinkle with pepper. Return to oven and bake, turning once, for another 8 minutes, until bacon is bubbling and coated. Set aside to cool on the baking sheet.

3. In a large bowl, arrange spinach and radishes. Toss with dressing. Top with bacon, blue cheese, and chives and serve.

Maple Balsamic Vinaigrette

This dressing is a culinary chameleon—it will highlight just about any combination of salad goodies you throw together. We love it best with baby spinach, fresh chèvre, toasted almonds, and dried cranberries. It's even better with a bit of bacon!

Makes 1¼ cups | Active time: 10 minutes | Total Time: 10 minutes

1   clove garlic

²/₃ cup best quality extra virgin olive oil

¹/₃ cup best quality balsamic vinegar

¼ cup dark pure maple syrup

2   teaspoons Dijon mustard

1   teaspoon salt

½ teaspoon freshly ground black pepper

1   teaspoon dried tarragon, optional

In a food processor, blender, or mini-prep, puree garlic, oil, vinegar, syrup, mustard, salt, and pepper for 25 to 35 seconds, until completely combined and emulsified. Stir in tarragon (if using).

Make ahead: Store in a tightly sealed jar in the refrigerator for up to 4 days. Before using, bring to room temperature and shake well to combine.

Orange Miso Dressing

This 5-minute dressing will turn a bowl of chopped cabbage or simple steamed fish into a delight. Choose your favorite oil for this one. I like a blend of good olive oil and flax oil.

Makes ⁷⁄₈ cup | Active time: 5 minutes | Total time: 5 minutes

1 teaspoon orange zest

2 tablespoons freshly squeezed orange juice

2 tablespoons dark pure maple syrup

1 tablespoon white vinegar

1 tablespoon miso paste, preferably white miso

1 tablespoon reduced-sodium soy sauce or or reduced-sodium, wheat-free tamari

½ teaspoon granulated garlic

¼ teaspoon freshly ground black pepper

⅓ cup extra-virgin olive oil or oil of choice

Ⓖ Gluten-free: Substitute wheat-free tamari for soy sauce.

In a medium bowl, whisk zest, juice, syrup, vinegar, miso, soy sauce, garlic, and pepper. Whisk in oil. Dress greens or salad.

Make ahead: Store in the refrigerator for up to 4 days in a tightly sealed jar.

Grainy Mustard Maple Vinaigrette

Much sharper than a typical honey mustard dressing, this maple-spiked version pairs well with bitter winter greens, salty meats, and sharp cheeses.

Makes 1 cup | Active time: 10 minutes | Total time: 10 minutes

1 small shallot, peeled, root removed, and quartered

⅓ cup extra virgin olive oil

¼ cup apple cider vinegar

2 tablespoons whole grain mustard

2 tablespoons dark pure maple syrup

½ teaspoon salt

¼ teaspoon freshly ground black pepper

In a food processor, blender, or mini prep, or with an immersion blender, puree all ingredients. Use immediately or refrigerate in a sealed jar for up to 1 week.

Make ahead: Store in the refrigerator for up to 1 week in a tightly sealed jar.

Maple Ranch Dressing

Ranch dressing (shown left) always has a touch of sugar to balance out the flavors. Why not get that sweetness from pure maple syrup? For a more overt maple flavor, choose a darker grade; for a less pronounced maple flavor and a more classic ranch taste, choose light amber.

Makes 8 2-tablespoon servings | Active time: 10 minutes | Total time: 10 minutes

½ cup plain low-fat Greek yogurt

2 tablespoons mayonnaise

2 tablespoons white wine vinegar

2 tablespoons chopped fresh chives

4 teaspoons pure maple syrup

1 tablespoon buttermilk powder (such as Saco) or nutritional yeast

½ teaspoon dried dill

½ teaspoon salt

¼ teaspoon freshly ground black pepper

In a blender or food processor, puree all ingredients. Use immediately or refrigerate in a sealed jar for up to 1 week.

Make ahead: Store in the refrigerator for up to 1 week in a tightly sealed jar.

Main Courses

When I first started writing maple recipes, one of the maple sugar makers I spoke to joked, "Do me a favor, don't include any recipes that call for only a teaspoon of maple." Well, we all should monitor our intake of added sugar. So the recipes in this chapter don't go overboard, but none calls for only a teaspoon of maple syrup! In these main dishes, the maple taste and sweetness highlight the savory flavors. The key is to provide contrast with a hint of spice, a splash of something sour, or a salty element.

Simple Miso Roasted Tofu

When it comes to tofu, you're either a fan or you're not. Even if you're not, try this recipe.
I'm betting it will change a few minds.

Makes 4 cups | Active time: 10 minutes | Total time: 55 minutes

2 tablespoons avocado oil or organic canola oil, divided

2 14-ounce packages extra-firm tofu packed in water, drained

3 tablespoons dark pure maple syrup

2 tablespoons miso paste

1 tablespoon white vinegar

½ teaspoon sriracha or hot sauce, or to taste

G Gluten-free: Use gluten-free miso paste.

1. Preheat oven to 425°F. Brush 1 tablespoon of the oil onto a rimmed baking sheet.

2. Pat tofu dry with clean paper towels. Cut into ¾-inch cubes. Toss in a large bowl with remaining 1 tablespoon oil and spread on the baking sheet in a single layer. Bake, turning every 10 to 15 minutes, for 30 to 35 minutes, until tofu is browned on most sides.

3. In the same bowl, whisk syrup, miso paste, vinegar, and sriracha. Drizzle over tofu and toss until coated. Spread in a single layer and continue roasting for another 2 to 3 minutes, until sauce is bubbling and starting to caramelize. Serve immediately.

Maple Wheat Pizza Dough

This pizza dough smells divine while it's baking and has just the right level of sweetness for a pizza. It favors toppings like smoked cheese, chopped woody herbs such as rosemary and thyme, caramelized onions, bacon, and winter squash. And, of course, garlic!

Makes about 1¼ pounds | Active time: 12 minutes | Total time: 2 hours

½ cup warm (105°F–115°F) water

1 package rapid or instant dry yeast

¼ cup maple syrup, warmed

1 tablespoon extra-virgin olive oil, plus more for bowl

¾ teaspoon salt

1½ cups white whole wheat flour

1 cup bread flour, divided, plus more for dusting

1. In a large mixing bowl, whisk water and yeast and let sit until foamy. Add syrup, oil, and salt and whisk to combine. Add whole wheat flour and ½ cup bread flour. Stir with a wooden spoon until too difficult to stir. Turn onto a floured surface and knead until dough comes together as a ball. Continue kneading, working the remaining 1½ cup bread flour into the dough, about 10 minutes, until dough is smooth and elastic. Alternatively, mix dough in a stand mixer fitted with the dough hook attachment for 5 to 6 minutes, until smooth and elastic and dough climbs the hook.

2. Coat a clean bowl with oil, set dough in bowl, cover with damp kitchen towel, and let rise in a warm spot for 1 to 2 hours, until almost doubled. Continue with the Balsamic Caramelized Onion Pizza (page 105) or your favorite pizza recipe.

Balsamic Caramelized Onion Pizza with Arugula and Maple Drizzle

I wish I could claim responsibility for coming up with the idea of drizzling maple on pizza. I first saw it on the menu of the local bakery of our little Vermont town. The syrup adds a lovely balance to the salty cheese. Trust me.

Makes 4 2-piece servings | Active time: 40 minutes | Total time: 55 minutes

1 tablespoon organic canola oil

1 large sweet onion, sliced

2 tablespoons balsamic vinegar

½ teaspoon chopped fresh thyme leaves

2 tablespoons cornmeal

All-purpose flour for dusting

Maple Wheat Pizza Dough (page 103), or your favorite store-bought dough

1 cup shredded sharp cheddar (4 ounces)

2 ounces crumbled feta, preferably reduced fat

2 tablespoons pepitas

¼ teaspoon salt

Freshly ground black pepper, to taste

3 cups loosely packed baby arugula (2 ounces)

2 tablespoons dark pure maple syrup

1. Place oil in a medium saucepan. Add onion, cover, and place over medium heat. Cook, stirring occasionally, 12 to 15 minutes, until onion is soft and starting to brown. Reduce heat to medium-low if they are browning too much before softening. Stir in vinegar and thyme, cover, remove from heat, and set aside while you prepare the pizza.

2. Place a rack in the bottom position of the oven. Preheat oven to 450°F. Coat a large rimmed baking sheet with nonstick cooking spray and sprinkle with cornmeal. Dust clean work surface with flour. Roll out dough to the size of the baking sheet and transfer to the sheet.

3. Spread caramelized onions over dough. Top with cheddar and feta. Sprinkle with pepitas, salt, and pepper.

4. Bake, rotating once halfway through, 13 to 16 minutes, until crust is crispy and cheese is bubbling and just starting to turn golden. Remove from oven. Scatter arugula over pizza and drizzle with syrup. Cut into 8 pieces and serve.

Maple Ginger Chicken Thighs

You know how some cookbooks automatically fall open to a particular page because you've used that recipe so many times? Mark my words, this will be that page. Here is a sweet, savory, and easy-as-heck recipe that is perfect for a chilly evening spent with friends.

Makes 8 servings | Active time: 15 minutes | Total time: 13 hours

1   shallot, finely sliced

¾   cup apple cider

½   cup dark pure maple syrup

1   tablespoon finely grated peeled, fresh ginger

1   tablespoon apple cider vinegar

1   teaspoon chopped fresh thyme leaves, plus four sprigs, divided

¾   teaspoon salt

½   teaspoon ground black pepper

8   bone-in chicken thighs

3   medium pears or apples, peeled, cored, and quartered

1. In a medium bowl, whisk shallot, cider, syrup, ginger, vinegar, thyme, salt, and pepper. Place chicken in a large resealable bag. Pour marinade into bag, seal it, and refrigerate for 12 to 24 hours, turning once or twice to agitate marinade and coat all pieces.

2. Preheat oven to 400°F. Remove chicken from marinade and arrange pieces, skin side up, in a 9-by-13-inch baking dish. Tuck pears and thyme sprigs among chicken pieces. Pour marinade over top. Bake, basting occasionally, about 1 hour, until chicken is cooked through and starting to pull from the bone. Serve chicken and pears with sauce spooned over top.

Vermonter Quesadillas with Maple Cream

What is it about Mondays that makes getting dinner on the table so hard? These quick Vermont-inspired quesadillas have become our go-to for just those kinds of nights.

Make 2 servings | Active time: 10 minutes | Total time: 20 minutes

2 tablespoons sour cream

2 tablespoons nonfat Greek yogurt

4 teaspoons dark pure maple syrup

Pinch ground chipotle, optional

2 8-inch tortillas, preferably whole wheat or multigrain

½ cup shredded sharp cheddar cheese (2 ounces)

½ apple, cored and thinly sliced

1. Make maple cream: In a small bowl, whisk sour cream, yogurt, syrup, and chipotle (if using).

2. Lay tortillas on a work surface. Divide cheese between them, covering only half of each circle. Top cheese with apple slices. Fold over tortillas.

3. Coat a large skillet with cooking spray and set over medium-high heat. Lay tortillas in the skillet, folded sides together. Cook for 4 to 6 minutes, until bottoms are browned. Flip quesadillas and continue cooking, adjusting heat as necessary to prevent burning, another 3 to 5 minutes, until bottoms are browned.

4. Slice and serve with the maple cream.

Chicken, Peanut, and Napa Cabbage Pad Thai

When I first described this book to a friend, she was confused that I would be including savory recipes. So I said, "You know how Pad Thai always includes a little bit of sugar? Well, I'll use maple syrup!" She instantly understood, and I knew then that I'd have to include a killer Thai recipe in the lineup. This one won't disappoint!

Makes 4 (generous) 2-cup servings | Active time: 30 minutes | Total time: 30 minutes

6 ounces rice noodles

3 tablespoons dark pure maple syrup

2 tablespoons tomato paste

2 tablespoons lime juice

2 tablespoons Thai fish sauce

1 tablespoon white vinegar

1 teaspoon sriracha

½ teaspoon salt

4 teaspoons avocado oil or organic canola oil

1 pound ground chicken or turkey

1 bunch scallions, sliced, white and green parts separated

8 cups chopped Napa cabbage (about 1 small head)

½ cup reduced-fat coconut milk

⅓ cup chopped roasted cashews or peanuts

2 tablespoons chopped cilantro

2 tablespoons chopped fresh basil, preferably Thai basil

1. Bring 4 cups of water to a boil in a kettle. Place noodles in a 9-by-13-inch baking dish. Pour enough boiling water to completely submerge noodles and swish them around a little to make sure they aren't sticking. Let soften for 10 minutes, agitating gently once or twice to prevent clumping. Drain and rinse noodles with cold water.

2. Meanwhile, in a small bowl, whisk syrup, tomato paste, juice, fish sauce, vinegar, sriracha, and salt. Set aside.

3. Heat oil in a large skillet over medium-high heat. Add meat and scallion whites. Stir with a wooden spoon to crumble meat as it browns. Cook for 6 to 9 minutes, until meat is cooked through. Add cabbage and coconut milk and reduce heat to medium. Stir for 1 to 2 minutes, until cabbage is slightly wilted. Transfer turkey mixture to a large bowl.

4. Add maple sauce and drained noodles to the skillet. Cook over medium heat, stirring, about 1 minute, until noodles are heated through. Transfer mixture to the bowl with the turkey, add scallion greens, and toss to coat. Serve topped with nuts and herbs.

Maple Tahini Chicken and Broccoli

This recipe has lived on my blog for ages, and it remains one of my—and my readers'—favorites! There is something transcendent about the balance of sweet and savory in the creamy tahini sauce. I love the way it soaks into the crisp, tender broccoli florets. Serve this dish with brown rice or whole grain noodles.

Makes 4 1½-cup servings | Active time: 40 minutes | Total time: 40 minutes

2 tablespoons dark pure maple syrup

2 tablespoons tahini

2 tablespoons reduced-sodium soy sauce or reduced-sodium, wheat-free tamari

2 teaspoons cornstarch

Pinch salt

4 teaspoons avocado oil or organic canola oil, divided

1 pound boneless skinless chicken breast, cubed

¼ teaspoon ground white pepper or black pepper

1 bunch scallions, sliced, white and green parts separated

2 teaspoons grated or minced peeled fresh ginger

1 cup reduced-sodium chicken broth

4 cups broccoli florets (about 2 small crowns)

2 cups peeled, sliced carrots

1 tablespoon lime juice

2 teaspoons sesame seeds for garnish, optional

G **Gluten-free:** Substitute wheat-free tamari for soy sauce.

1. In a small bowl, whisk syrup, tahini, soy sauce, cornstarch, and salt; set aside.

2. Place large skillet over high heat. Add 2 teaspoons oil and swirl to coat skillet. Add chicken, sprinkle with pepper, and cook, turning once or twice, 5 to 6 minutes, until browned. (Note: the chicken will not be fully cooked at this stage; it will continue cooking in the sauce in step 4.) Transfer chicken to a plate and set aside.

3. Add remaining 2 teaspoons oil to the skillet, followed by scallion whites and ginger. Cook, stirring, 15 to 30 seconds, until fragrant. Add broth and bring to a simmer, scraping up browned bits. Add broccoli and carrots, cover, and simmer, stirring once or twice, 4 to 5 minutes, until broccoli is bright green and vegetables are still crisp but softening slightly.

4. Stir sauce, chicken, and accumulated juices from the chicken plate into vegetables and continue cooking, stirring often, 4 to 5 minutes, until chicken is cooked through and sauce is thickened. Remove from heat. Stir in reserved scallion greens, lime juice, and sesame seeds (if using) and serve.

Turkey Burgers with Maple Pickled Onions

A topping made with sweet 'n' tart onions and gooey melted cheese takes burger night from blah to terrific. If you can't find fontina, substitute with a good monterey jack.

Makes 4 servings; 1 cup of onions | Active time: 20 minutes | Total time: 40 minutes

½ cup red wine vinegar

¼ cup dark pure maple syrup

1 tablespoon pickling spice*

1 teaspoon salt, divided

   Freshly ground black pepper, to taste

1 small red onion, peeled and thinly sliced (preferably with a mandolin)

1 pound ground lean turkey

2 ounces (about ½ cup) shredded fontina cheese

4 burger buns, preferably whole wheat, toasted if desired

4 leaves green leaf lettuce, washed and patted dry

  This blend of whole dried spices is used in pickles and many canning recipes. Blends vary by brand but often include allspice berries, bay leaf, and mustard seeds. Sold in the spice section of supermarkets or the bulk section of health food stores.

1. In a small saucepan, bring to a simmer vinegar, syrup, pickling spice, ¾ teaspoon salt, and pepper. Stir over high heat and boil for 2 minutes.

2. Place onion in a medium heatproof bowl or measuring cup. Strain hot vinegar mixture through a fine-mesh sieve over onions and toss with a fork. Discard solids in sieve. Let onions cool in pickling liquid, stirring 2 or 3 times, about 30 minutes, until mixture reaches room temperature. Use immediately or refrigerate onions in their liquid up to 1 week.

3. Meanwhile, preheat grill to medium-high heat. Form turkey into 4 thin patties. Sprinkle both sides of each patty with remaining ¼ teaspoon salt and pepper. Oil grill rack and immediately arrange burgers. Grill for 4 to 5 minutes, until cooked about halfway. Flip, top each burger with cheese, and continue cooking for another 4 to 5 minutes, until meat is cooked through and no longer pink. Serve on buns. Top with lettuce and onions.

How to Oil a Grill Rack

Soak a paper towel or clean kitchen rag with avocado oil or canola oil. Hold the towel with tongs and rub it over the grill rack, pulling toward you. Do not use cooking spray on a hot grill.

Ham and Cheddar Monte Cristo Sandwiches with Raspberry Maple Syrup

Monte Cristo sandwiches always make me think of my grandmother, who never failed to order one if it was a menu option. Instead of the traditional raspberry jam, I serve these fork-and-knife versions doused with warm maple syrup enhanced with fresh raspberries.

Makes 4 servings; ¼ cup of sauce | Active time: 20 minutes | Total time: 20 minutes

1 cup fresh or frozen and thawed raspberries

¼ cup dark pure maple syrup

6 large eggs

2 tablespoons water

4 teaspoons organic canola oil, divided

8 slices hearty multigrain bread

8 ounces thinly sliced smoked ham

1 cup (4 ounces) shredded sharp cheddar cheese

1. In a small saucepan, bing raspberries and syrup to a boil. Simmer, stirring occasionally, 1 to 3 minutes, until raspberries soften. Remove from heat and mash with a fork. Cover and set aside.

2. Preheat oven to 300°F. Place a wire rack on a large baking sheet and set aside.

3. Use a whisk to beat eggs and water in a shallow baking dish. Heat 1 teaspoon oil in a large skillet over medium heat. Once the pan is hot, reduce heat to medium-low to prevent scorching. Dip 2 slices of bread into egg mixture and flip to coat. Swirl oil to coat the bottom of the skillet. Allow excess egg to drip off bread and place in the skillet. Cook for 1 to 3 minutes, until browned on the bottom. Flip slices with a spatula. Layer a quarter of the ham and 1 ounce cheese on one bread slice. Cook for 1 to 2 minutes, until bread is browned on the bottom and cheese starts to melt. Place second bread slice on top of the ham and cheese.

4. Transfer sandwich to the prepared rack. Place the baking sheet in the oven to keep sandwich warm.

5. Repeat with the remaining bread and ingredients, using a teaspoon of oil for each batch. Slice sandwiches in half and serve with warm raspberry syrup.

Asian Pork Cabbage Cups

My husband has a real love for food he can eat with his hands, so he's a big fan of this dish. I love it for the balance of sweet and gingery flavors. If you don't like cabbage, try Bibb lettuce.

Makes 4 servings (each 1 cup pork and 3 cabbage leaves) | Active time: 25 minutes |
Total time: 25 minutes

2 teaspoons avocado oil or organic canola oil

1 pound ground pork, preferably natural heritage

4 scallions, thinly sliced, white and green parts separated

1 tablespoon minced or finely grated and peeled fresh ginger

2 tablespoons reduced-sodium soy sauce; reduced-sodium, wheat-free tamari; or Thai fish sauce

2 tablespoons dark pure maple syrup

1 tablespoon white vinegar

1 teaspoon toasted sesame oil

¼ teaspoon salt

½ cup julienned snow peas

½ cup julienned carrots, julienned or shredded (about 1 medium carrot)

½ cup julienned radishes (about 6 large radishes)

¼ cup chopped roasted unsalted cashews

2 tablespoons chopped fresh basil, cilantro, or a mixture

12 savoy cabbage leaves, washed and dried

G **Gluten-free:** Substitute wheat-free tamari for soy sauce.

P **Paleo-friendly:** Substitute 4 teaspoons Thai fish sauce for soy sauce.

1. Heat oil in a large heavy skillet over high heat until shimmering but not smoking. Add pork, scallion whites, and ginger. Reduce heat to medium-high and cook, stirring often and breaking up meat, 7 to 10 minutes, until meat is just cooked through and no longer pink. Remove from heat and stir in soy sauce.

2. In a large bowl, whisk syrup, vinegar, sesame oil, and salt. Stir in pork mixture. Stir in snow peas, carrots, radishes, cashews, scallion greens, and basil.

3. Place 3 cabbage leaves curved side up on each of 4 plates. Divide pork salad among them, using about ⅓ cup mixture per cabbage cup. Serve.

Sap-Braised Pulled Pork with Maple Chipotle Barbecue Sauce

When the sap is running, there's always a crowd to feed around here, and that's why I came up with this method for slow-cooking pork for sandwiches. Make sure to serve it with all the classic accompaniments, like Sweet and Sour Coleslaw (page 84) and plenty of cold beer.

Makes 8½-cup servings | Active time: 40 minutes | Total time: 5 hours

2 teaspoons avocado oil or organic canola oil, divided

3 pounds bone-in pork butt or picnic shoulder

3 cups diced onion

1 tablespoon finely chopped garlic

1 teaspoon salt, divided

1 cup light-bodied beer, such as pilsner or lager

4 cups filtered or strained maple sap*

3 teaspoons smoked paprika, divided

½ teaspoon ground black pepper

1 6-ounce can tomato paste

⅓ cup maple syrup

¼ cup apple cider vinegar

2 tablespoons coarse ground mustard or brown mustard

1 teaspoon ground dried chipotle

½ teaspoon onion powder

If unavailable, substitute 4 cups water mixed with 3 tablespoons dark pure maple syrup.

1. Heat 1 teaspoon oil in a large skillet over medium-high heat. Add pork and sear for 7 to 9 minutes, until browned. Flip and continue searing for another 5 to 6 minutes, until meat is browned on the bottom. Transfer pork to a slow cooker. Pour off fat from the skillet.

2. Add remaining 1 teaspoon oil, onion, garlic, and ½ teaspoon salt to the skillet. Cook over medium-high heat, stirring, 3 to 5 minutes, until onion starts to soften and brown.

3. Add beer, bring to a simmer, and scrape up any browned bits from the skillet bottom. Transfer to slow cooker. Add sap, 2 teaspoons paprika, and black pepper to the slow cooker.

4. In a small bowl, whisk tomato paste, syrup, vinegar, mustard, chipotle, onion powder, the remaining 1 teaspoon paprika, and the remaining ½ teaspoon salt. Set aside ¾ cup of the resulting barbecue sauce. Stir remaining 1/2 cup sauce into the slow cooker. Cover and cook for 4 hours on high.

5. Transfer meat to a cutting board. Remove bones and large pieces of fat. Shred meat with two forks. Skim fat off the liquid in the slow cooker and discard; moisten meat with a little of the braising liquid.

6. Serve pork with the reserved ¾ cup barbecue sauce.

Sweet and Sour Cabbage Rolls

You could almost call this recipe Sloppy Joe Cabbage Rolls, so much does the mix resemble the flavor of that dish. To remove the cabbage leaves whole, try coring the head with a sharp paring knife. But don't worry if the leaves tear; just cook a few extras and wrap two together.

Makes 4 2-roll servings | Active time: 30 minutes | Total time: 50 minutes

8 whole leaves from 1 large cabbage

3 cups boiling water

1 tablespoon extra-virgin olive oil

1 large onion, diced

¼ teaspoon salt

½ pound (preferably grass fed) lean ground beef

1 cup finely chopped mushrooms

½ teaspoon ground black pepper

3 tablespoons tomato paste

3 tablespoons red wine vinegar

3 tablespoons dark pure maple syrup

2 teaspoons Worcestershire sauce

1 15-ounce can tomato sauce, (about 1¾ cups)

1 cup shredded part-skim mozzarella

1. Stack cabbage leaves in a large Dutch oven and pour boiling water over top. Cover, set over high heat, and boil, rotating top leaves to the bottom as the stack shrinks. Cook for 4 to 6 minutes, until cabbage is just tender enough to be pliable, but not so soft that it tears. Drain and lay leaves on a work surface to cool.

2. Heat oil in a large nonstick skillet over medium-high heat. Add onion and salt and cook, stirring often, 6 to 8 minutes, until onion is soft, translucent, and starting to brown. Add beef, mushrooms, and pepper and cook, breaking up with a wooden spoon, 3 to 4 minutes, until beef is browned and no pink remains. Add tomato paste and stir until beef and onion are coated and paste is not clumpy. Add vinegar, syrup, and Worcestershire sauce and bring to a simmer, stirring often. Remove from heat.

3. Spoon ¼ cup filling onto each cabbage leaf and roll, tucking in the sides. Arrange rolls in the skillet side by side, seam side down. Pour tomato sauce over rolls. Cover and place over medium-low heat. Cook in the simmering sauce for about 20 minutes, until rolls are heated through and cabbage is tender. Remove lid and sprinkle with mozzarella. Cover and cook for 1 to 2 minutes, until cheese melts. Let rolls sit for 10 minutes before serving.

Maple Pork Loin Roast with Apple Chutney

Pork loin has a reputation for being dry and boring, but this cider and maple brine makes it anything but. Try it with Sweet and Sour Skillet Sauerkraut (page 85) and roasted root vegetables.

Makes 6 servings (each 4 ounces of pork and ¼ cup of chutney) | Active time: 25 minutes | Total time: 6 hours 30 minutes

BRINE

2 cups apple cider

½ cup dark pure maple syrup

4 bay leaves

1 sprig rosemary

1 teaspoon ground cinnamon

⅓ cup kosher salt

3 cups ice

1 2-pound boneless pork loin roast

APPLE CHUTNEY

2 teaspoons unsalted butter

1 shallot, minced

2 tablespoons apple cider vinegar

2 tablespoons dark pure maple syrup

½ teaspoon mustard seeds

½ teaspoon salt

2 sweet, firm apples, such as Golden Delicious or Cortland, peeled and diced

MAPLE SUGAR RUB

1 tablespoon maple sugar

1 tablespoon softened unsalted butter

1 teaspoon brown mustard

½ teaspoon chopped fresh rosemary

½ teaspoon freshly ground black pepper

¼ teaspoon salt

1. Whisk cider and syrup in a medium saucepan. Add bay leaves, rosemary, and cinnamon and set over high heat. Bring to a simmer, stirring occasionally. Stir in salt until dissolved and remove from heat. Stir in ice. Brine should be at room temperature or colder.

2. Tie pork with butcher's twine in several places to hold a round shape. Place in a deep bowl or resealable bag set in a bowl. Cover pork with cider brine. Reseal bag and cover bowl. Refrigerate for 4 to 6 hours.

3. In a medium saucepan, melt butter over medium heat. Add shallot and cook, stirring often, 30 to 90 seconds, until fragrant and starting to brown. Add vinegar, syrup, mustard seeds, and salt. Increase heat to high and bring to a simmer, stirring often. Stir in apples to coat, cover, and cook, stirring occasionally, 4 to 6 minutes, until apples soften and start to break down.

4. Preheat oven to 425°F. Remove pork and discard brine; pat meat dry with paper towels.

5. In a small dish, mix maple sugar, butter, and mustard. Add rosemary, pepper, and salt and stir to form a paste. Spread over pork and set it in a small roasting pan.

6. Roast pork for 38 to 45 minutes, until a thermometer inserted into the center of the roast reaches 145°F. Let rest on a carving board for 15 minutes before removing twine and slicing.

Maple Mustard Potatoes with Sausage and Apples

This is one of those clean-plate-club weeknight standbys that I make throughout the cold months. If there are ever leftovers, they are great warmed up for lunch the next day.

Make 4 2-cup servings | Active time: 15 minutes | Total time: 45 minutes

2 pounds (about 6 cups) small red, blue, or gold potatoes, cut into 1-inch chunks

1 tablespoon extra-virgin olive oil

1 teaspoon kosher salt

½ teaspoon freshly ground black pepper

4 links (12 ounces) fully cooked chicken sausage, sliced in ½-inch pieces

2 Golden Delicious apples, peeled, cored, and cut into 1½-inch chunks

3 tablespoons dark pure maple syrup

2 tablespoons whole grain mustard

1½ tablespoons apple cider vinegar or red wine vinegar

1. Preheat oven to 450°F.

2. In a large bowl, toss potatoes, oil, salt, and pepper until coated. Spread potatoes in a large, heavy roasting pan. Roast for 10 minutes. Meanwhile, in a large bowl, stir sausage, apples, syrup, mustard, and vinegar.

3. Remove roasting pan from oven. Reduce oven temperature to 375°F. Stir potatoes with a spatula, scraping up any stuck to the pan. Add sausage mixture to potatoes and toss to combine. Return to the oven and bake, stirring once or twice, 30 to 35 minutes, until potatoes and apples are tender and glaze is caramelized. Serve warm.

Chipotle and Maple Flank Steak Tacos with Zippy Cabbage Slaw

If you ask me, chipotle and maple are a match made in heaven. Here, they come together to tame the bold gaminess of grass-fed beef. Ice-cold beer is a must with these festive, brightly hued tacos.

Makes 6 2-taco servings | Active time: 30 minutes | Total time: 12½ hours

3 chipotle peppers in adobo sauce, minced

¼ cup plus 2 teaspoons dark pure maple syrup

5 tablespoons apple cider vinegar, divided

1½ teaspoons salt, divided

1 small grass-fed flank steak (about 1½ pounds)

2 teaspoons organic canola oil

3 cups finely chopped cabbage (about ½ small cabbage)

½ cup julienned radishes

¼ cup roughly chopped cilantro leaves

12 6-inch corn tortillas, warmed

1 avocado, diced

1. In a small bowl, whisk peppers, ¼ cup syrup, 3 tablespoons vinegar, and 1 teaspoon salt. Place flank steak in a large resealable plastic bag. Add pepper mixture. Reseal and turn to coat. Refrigerate for 12 to 24 hours.

2. Preheat grill to medium-high heat. Remove steak and discard remaining marinade. Oil grill rack. Grill steaks for 5 to 7 minutes per side for medium rare, 6 to 7 minutes for medium, or 8 minutes per side for medium well. Let rest for 10 minutes while preparing slaw.

3. In a medium bowl, whisk remaining 2 teaspoons syrup, remaining 2 tablespoons vinegar, remaining ½ teaspoon salt, and oil. Add cabbage, radishes, and cilantro and toss to combine. Slice flank steak into thin strips, across the grain. Fill tortillas with steak and slaw, top with avocado, and serve.

Spicy Peanut Noodles with White Pepper Sirloin

For the longest time, I thought I hated white pepper. It has a slightly funky flavor that I found all wrong. But then I discovered that it's one of the main flavors in hot-and-sour soup. I had in fact been enjoying it for a long time, and my perspective completely changed. Now I love to add it to Asian-inspired recipes or pair it with cheese, eggs, and other creamy dishes. Here, it dusts sirloin steak that's seared in a hot skillet. The sliced steak is piled on top of peanut noodles that have a sriracha kick and an orange surprise.

Makes 4 servings (each 1½ cup of noodles and 3 ounces of steak) | Active time: 35 minutes | Total time: 35 minutes

10 ounces whole wheat spaghetti

2 cups snow peas, cut in half

1¼ teaspoon kosher salt, divided

¼ teaspoon ground white pepper

1 (1-pound) sirloin steak, preferably grass-fed, ¾ inch- to 1 inch-thick

2 teaspoons peanut oil

¼ cup smooth natural peanut butter

Zest and juice of 1 orange

2 tablespoons dark pure maple syrup

2 teaspoons white vinegar

1 teaspoon sriracha, or more to taste

¼ cup chopped roasted unsalted peanuts

¼ cup sliced scallions

¼ cup chopped cilantro

1. Bring a large pot of water to a boil. Cook pasta according to package directions. Add snow peas for last minute of cooking. Reserve 1 cup cooking liquid. Drain pasta and snow peas, return to pot, cover, and set aside.

2. Meanwhile, combine ½ teaspoon salt and white pepper and sprinkle over steak. Heat oil in a medium heavy-bottomed skillet over high heat until oil is shimmering but not smoking. Add steak, reduce heat to medium-high, and cook until meat is browned, 3–4 minutes per side for medium-rare and 5–6 minutes per side for medium well. Let steak rest for at least 5 minutes. Use a sharp carving knife to slice against the grain into ¼- to ½-inch-thick strips, discarding large fat pieces.

3. Meanwhile, in a large bowl, whisk peanut butter, zest and juice, syrup, vinegar, sriracha, and remaining ¾ teaspoon salt until smooth and thick.

4. Add pasta and snow peas to peanut butter mixture and toss to combine. If noodles seem dry, add reserved pasta water ¼ cup at a time to loosen. Divide noodles among 4 bowls and top with steak. Garnish with peanuts, scallions, and cilantro and serve.

Maple Ginger Roasted Salmon

This easy-as-can-be dish is great for entertaining. It is certainly no wallflower when it comes to flavor! Pair it with steamed green and wax beans and brown rice. Store leftovers in the reduction overnight; the salmon will take on even more flavor and is wonderful served cold atop a salad.

Makes 6 servings | Active time: 15 minutes | Total time: 1 hour

¼ cup reduced-sodium soy sauce or reduced-sodium, wheat-free tamari

¼ cup dark pure maple syrup

1 tablespoon white vinegar

1 tablespoon grated and peeled fresh ginger

½ teaspoon crushed red pepper, optional

1 1¾- to 2-pound boneless side of wild salmon, skin on

 Gluten-free: Substitute wheat-free tamari for soy sauce.

1. In a large baking dish, stir soy sauce, syrup, vinegar, ginger, and red pepper. Lay salmon skin side up in marinade and refrigerate, covered, 30 minutes to 1 hour.

2. Preheat oven to 425°F. Line a large roasting pan or rimmed baking sheet with foil.

3. Lay salmon on the foil, skin side down. Roast, uncovered, until fish is barely cooked in the center, about 9 to 13 minutes for medium well.

4. Meanwhile, pour marinade into a small saucepan and bring to a simmer over medium-high heat. Simmer for 6 to 9 minutes, until thick and syrupy. Pour reduction over fish before serving.

Hot Pepper Fish Cakes with Herb Salad

Sweet, sour, salty, and a touch of bitter: these fish cakes and fresh salad have it all. It's like an explosion of taste and flavors.

Makes 4 servings (each 2 cakes and 1 cup salad) | Active time: 35 minutes | Total time: 35 minutes

1 pound tilapia, haddock, or barramundi fillet, cut into large chunks

1 tablespoon cornstarch

1 teaspoon lime zest

2 tablespoons plus 2 teaspoons Thai fish sauce, divided

1 tablespoon plus 2 teaspoons amber or dark pure maple syrup, divided

1 tablespoon grated fresh galangal or 2 teaspoons peeled and grated fresh ginger

1 teaspoon minced fresh chile, preferably Thai chile, or 1/4 teaspoon crushed red pepper flakes

2 tablespoons coconut oil, divided

3 tablespoons lime juice

1 tablespoon avocado oil or organic canola oil

Freshly ground black pepper

4 cups shredded romaine lettuce or napa cabbage

1 scallion, minced

1 cup julienned radishes (about 6 large radishes)

1 loosely packed cup torn mixture of basil, cilantro, and mint leaves (any combination)

1. Coat a baking sheet with nonstick cooking spray.

2. Place fish in food processor with cornstarch, zest, 2 tablespoons fish sauce, 1 tablespoon syrup, galangal, and chile. Pulse until mixture forms a rough, sticky dough. Moisten hands and form 8½-inch-thick patties. (Use about ¼ cup fish mixture for each patty.) Place patties on baking sheet.

3. In a large skillet, heat 1 tablespoon coconut oil over medium-high heat. Add half the fish patties and cook, uncovered, 2 to 4 minutes, until browned on the bottom. Carefully flip and continue cooking, adjusting heat as necessary to prevent burning, 2 to 3 minutes, until cooked through and browned on the other side. Transfer to a paper-towel-lined plate; tent with foil to keep warm. Repeat with remaining 1 tablespoon coconut oil and fish patties.

4. Whisk remaining 2 teaspoons fish sauce, 2 teaspoons syrup, lime juice, oil, and pepper in a large bowl. Add lettuce, scallion, radishes, and herbs and toss to coat. Divide salad among 4 plates, top with fish cakes, drizzle with remaining dressing from the bowl, and serve.

Swordfish with Maple Pipérade

During late summer, you'll find me stockpiling sweet peppers. I call it pepper fever. Pipérade is one of my favorite ways to prepare them. To make this dolled-up swordfish a meal, serve with angel hair pasta or whole wheat couscous to sop up the sweet-and-sour sauce.

Makes 4 servings (each 3½ ounces of fish and ⅔ cup of pipérade) | Active time: 20 minutes | Total time: 25 minutes

1 tablespoon plus 2 teaspoons extra-virgin olive oil, divided

2 large bell peppers, sliced

1 small shallot, sliced

1 pound boneless swordfish, about ½ inch thick, cut into 4 portions

¾ teaspoon coarse kosher salt

3 tablespoons red wine vinegar

2 tablespoons dark pure maple syrup

1 tablespoon capers

½ cup chopped fresh parsley

Freshly ground black pepper to taste

1. In a large nonstick skillet, heat 1 tablespoon oil over medium-high heat. Add peppers and shallot and cook, stirring often, 7 to 9 minutes, until peppers are crisp tender. Scrape mixture into a bowl and set aside.

2. Wipe skillet and return to medium-high heat. Add remaining 2 teaspoons oil and swirl in the pan. Add swordfish and sprinkle with salt. Cook for 2 to 4 minutes, until browned on the bottom. Flip fish and pour vinegar and syrup over top. Top fish with pepper mixture and sprinkle with capers. Continue cooking for another 3 minutes, until fish is just barely cooked through.

3. Use a slotted spatula to transfer fish and peppers to 4 plates. Increase heat to high and reduce sauce for 1 to 3 minutes, stirring once or twice, until thickened and syrupy. Drizzle over fish and peppers. Serve sprinkled with parsley and pepper.

Desserts

My grandmother, a lover of sweets and a stickler for perfect spelling, once shared her trick for remembering the difference between dessert and desert: "When it comes to dessert, I'll take two." In the case of the following recipes, I wonder if she would have made an exception for spelling errors that included an extra "s."

Hazelnut Maple Thumbprint Cookies with Maple Butter

The first time I made these cookies, I brought a few up the hill to my neighbor Jack, an experienced sugar maker. His opinion on all things maple is as good as gold! He gave them his seal of approval and added that he would be happy to serve as taste tester for any future batches.

Makes about 35 cookies | Active time: 45 minutes | Total time: 2 hours 10 minutes

¾ cup whole hazelnuts (about 3½ ounces)

2 tablespoons granulated sugar

1 cup white whole wheat flour

¾ cup all-purpose flour

1 teaspoon baking powder

½ teaspoon salt

½ cup unsalted butter, softened

¾ cup maple sugar

1 egg

2 teaspoons vanilla extract

¼ cup maple butter (also called maple cream)

1. In food processor, process hazelnuts and sugar for about 40 seconds, until finely ground. Scrape the bowl sides with a spatula. Add flours, baking powder, and salt and pulse to combine. Set aside.

2. Beat butter with an electric mixer on medium speed for about 1½ minutes, until light, fluffy, and smooth. Add maple sugar and beat until combined. Add egg and vanilla extract and beat until completely incorporated. Add hazelnut mixture and beat until just combined. Refrigerate dough for at least 20 minutes, or until firm.

3. While dough chills, place a rack in the center of the oven. Preheat oven to 350°F. Line two baking sheets with parchment paper.

4. Form 20 1-tablespoon scoops of dough into balls; refrigerate remaining dough. Arrange balls on a prepared baking sheet. Gently press the center of each with your thumb, creating a slight indent.

5. Bake, rotating the tray once halfway through, 10 to 12 minutes, until cookies are lightly golden. Repeat step 4 with remaining dough, forming about 15 more balls.

6. Allow cookies to cool before spooning a small dollop of maple butter into the center of each.

Make ahead: Batter can be froze for up to 1 month.

Maple Walnut Chocolate Chunk Cookies

Crispy on the edges, chewy on the inside, and lightly fragrant of maple, these cookies are nearly perfect.

Makes 28–30 cookies | Active time: 25 minutes | Total time: 1 hour

½ cup unsalted butter, softened

1 cup maple sugar, gently packed

1 large egg

2 tablespoons avocado oil or organic canola oil

2 teaspoons vanilla extract

1 cup whole wheat pastry flour

½ cup all-purpose flour

1 teaspoon baking soda

1 teaspoon baking powder

¼ teaspoon salt

1 cup dark chocolate chunks, chocolate chips, or white chocolate chips

1 cup toasted chopped walnuts

1. Arrange two racks in the upper and lower thirds of the oven, evenly spaced from the top and bottom. Preheat oven to 375°F. Coat two large baking sheets with nonstick cooking spray.

2. In a large bowl, use an electric mixer on medium speed to beat butter and maple sugar until creamy. Beat in egg. Beat in oil and vanilla. Scrape the bowl sides with a spatula.

3. In a medium bowl, whisk flours, baking soda, baking powder, and salt. Add flour mixture to butter mixture, stirring until just combined. Add chocolate chips and walnuts and stir to incorporate.

4. Drop dough by heaping tablespoons onto the prepared baking sheets, evenly spaced to allow for spreading, about 8 or 9 cookies per sheet. Bake 2 sheets at a time, rotating top to bottom and turning each sheet front to back once halfway through, 9 to 11 minutes, until cookies are puffed and starting to brown. Let cool on the baking sheet for 3 to 5 minutes. Transfer to a wire rack to cool completely before serving. Repeat with the remaining dough, cleaning and respraying baking sheets as necessary.

Maple Walnut Cookie Bars with Raisins

These bars have a texture similar to pecan pie, with a crumbly crust and a sweet, gooey filling.

Makes 16 bars | Active time: 30 minutes | Total time: 3 hours

- 2 cups walnut halves, divided
- 1 tablespoon maple sugar or granulated sugar
- ¾ cup whole wheat pastry flour
- 3 tablespoons plus 1½ teaspoons all-purpose flour, divided
- ½ teaspoon salt, divided
- 2 eggs plus 1 egg yolk, divided
- 2 tablespoons unsalted butter, melted, divided
- 3 tablespoons avocado oil or organic canola oil
- 3 tablespoons cold water
- ½ cup dark pure maple syrup
- 2 teaspoons apple cider vinegar
- 2 teaspoons vanilla extract
- 1 cup raisins

1. Preheat oven to 400°F. Coat an 8-by-8-inch baking dish with nonstick cooking spray.

2. In a food processor fitted with steel blade attachment, process ½ cup walnuts and maple sugar until mixture is the consistency of rough meal. Add pastry flour, 3 tablespoons all-purpose flour, and ¼ teaspoon salt and pulse until combined.

3. In a small bowl, stir 1 egg yolk, 1 tablespoon melted butter, and oil. With the food processor running, slowly pour yolk mixture through the feed tube and process until completely combined. Also with the food processor running, drizzle in water and then pulse until mixture just clumps together.

4. Spread batter evenly into prepared baking dish with a spatula, pressing firmly to form a crust. Prick all over with a fork. Bake for 10 to 13 minutes, until dry with slightly golden edges. If crust puffs during baking, press it with the back of a fork.

5. Meanwhile, in a medium bowl, whisk syrup, vinegar, vanilla, remaining ¼ teaspoon salt, remaining 2 eggs, and remaining 1 tablespoon butter. Set aside ¼ cup of the maple mixture.

6. Chop ½ cup of the walnuts and add to the bowl with the larger amount of maple mixture. Stir in raisins. Add remaining 1 cup walnuts to the ¼ cup maple mixture. Stir to coat.

7. Remove crust and reduce oven temperature to 350°F. Use a pastry brush to dab hot crust with remaining 1½ teaspoons flour, filling any holes or cracks. Spread with raisin mixture. Arrange walnut halves decoratively over top. Drizzle with remaining maple mixture. Bake for 30 to 35 minutes, until the center no longer jiggles when gently shaken, the top is lightly crackled, and the filling is set. Cool completely, at least 2 hours, before cutting into 16 squares. Store in a sealed container for up to 4 days.

Maple Apricot Hermit Cookies

A cookie-jar must! Bread flour and a bit of extra mixing give these golden-studded cookies their signature chewy texture.

Makes 24 cookies | Active time: 15 minutes | Total time: 2 hours

1 cup bread flour

½ cup white whole wheat flour

1 teaspoon baking soda

1 teaspoon ground cinnamon

½ teaspoon ground nutmeg

¼ teaspoon ground cloves

¼ teaspoon salt

1 cup chopped dried apricots

¾ cup maple sugar*

½ cup avocado oil or organic canola oil

⅓ cup unsulphured molasses

½ cup reduced-fat milk, almond milk, or soy milk

4 teaspoons turbinado sugar

* *If unavailable, use 1 cup dark pure maple syrup and increase bread flour to 1 cup plus 1 tablespoon. Cookies will be more cakey but still delicious.*

V Vegan: Substitute almond milk for reduced-fat milk.

1. Preheat oven to 350°F. Coat a 9-by-13-inch metal baking pan with nonstick cooking spray.

2. In a large bowl, whisk flours, baking soda, cinnamon, nutmeg, cloves, and salt until combined. Stir in apricots. Set aside.

3. In a separate medium bowl, whisk maple sugar, oil, molasses, and milk. Stir dry ingredients into wet ingredients until fully combined. Continue mixing for 50 strokes. Scrape into prepared pan. Use a spatula to spread batter evenly, ensuring that apricots are equally distributed.

4. Bake for 24 to 28 minutes, until puffed and a toothpick inserted into the center comes out clean. Remove from the oven and immediately sprinkle with turbinado sugar.

5. Let cool completely before cutting into 24 squares. Layer cookies between pieces of parchment paper inside a resealable container. Store at room temperature for 3 days or freeze for up to 1 month.

Maple Shortbread Cookies

When I asked my neighbor to sample these one afternoon, she said they were possibly the best cookies she'd ever eaten. I decided I'd better not tamper with the recipe too much after that.

Makes 18 cookies | Active time: 30 minutes | Total time: 2 hours

½ cup unsalted butter (1 stick)

½ cup maple sugar

1 egg yolk

1 cup all-purpose flour

1 teaspoon baking powder

¾ teaspoon salt

2¼ teaspoons turbinado sugar, optional

1. In a large bowl, beat butter and maple sugar with an electric mixer on medium speed until creamy and smooth. Beat in yolk until fully incorporated.

2. In a medium bowl, whisk flour, baking powder, and salt. Add flour mixture to butter mixture and beat for about 20 seconds, until a smooth dough comes together. Pat dough on the counter to form a 1-by-2-by-7-inch brick. Wrap in plastic and refrigerate dough for at least 4 hours, until completely chilled.

3. Preheat oven to 375°F. Use a sharp knife to cut half the dough into ¼-inch-thick slices. Refrigerate remaining dough. Arrange slices on the baking sheet, spacing them generously. Sprinkle with ⅛ teaspoon turbinado sugar (if using) per cookie. Bake for 8 to 10 minutes, until slightly browned. Remove from the oven. Let cool on the baking sheet for 5 minutes before transferring cookies to a cooling rack to cool completely. Repeat with remaining dough.

Cheesecake Swirl Brownies

Beware—these fudgy brownies may glue your mouth shut! But if you're a chocoholic like me, this is a wonderful predicament to be in.

Makes 24 brownies | Active time: 20 minutes | Total time: 5 hours

4 ounces Neufchâtel or reduced-fat cream cheese, room temperature

1 cup dark pure maple syrup, divided

2 eggs, divided

3 teaspoons vanilla extract, divided

⅔ cup all-purpose flour

½ cup cocoa powder, sifted

1 teaspoon baking powder

½ teaspoon baking soda, sifted

¼ teaspoon salt

¼ cup unsalted butter, melted

3 tablespoons avocado oil or organic canola oil

4 ounces bittersweet chocolate chips or chopped bittersweet chocolate, melted and cooled slightly*

½ cup nonfat buttermilk

Place chocolate in a small microwave-safe container. Microwave in 30-second bursts, stirring between each round, until mostly melted. Let sit, stirring often, until completely melted.

1. Preheat oven to 350°F. Coat a 9-by-13-inch baking pan with nonstick cooking spray.

2. In a large bowl, beat Neufchâtel and ¼ cup syrup with an electric mixer on high speed, scraping the bowl sides as necessary, until completely smooth. Add 1 egg and 1 teaspoon vanilla and beat, scraping the bowl sides as necessary, until smooth. Set aside.

3. In a medium bowl, whisk flour, cocoa powder, baking powder, baking soda, and salt. In a large bowl, beat butter, oil, chocolate, remaining ¾ cup syrup, remaining egg, and remaining 2 teaspoons vanilla on medium-high speed until completely smooth. Add flour mixture and beat on low speed until smooth. Add buttermilk and beat until completely combined.

4. Spread two-thirds of the chocolate mixture into the pan. Top with the maple cream cheese layer. Dot with remaining chocolate mixture and drag a clean knife through the layers to swirl.

5. Bake for 30 to 32 minutes, until brownie is set and edges are lightly puffed. Cool to room temperature on a wire rack. Refrigerate until chilled for the best texture. Cut into 24 brownies. Bring brownies to room temperature to serve. Store covered in the refrigerator for up to 4 days.

Maple Bananas Foster Bundt Cake

This ooey-gooey banana cake is a true showstopper. For extra drama, pour the hot maple over the cake when you serve it.

Makes 16 servings | Active time: 45 minutes | Total time: 4 hours

⅓ cup chopped pecans

¼ cup maple sugar

6 tablespoons butter, melted, divided

3 bananas, sliced into 1½-inch disks, plus ¾ cup mashed ripe bananas (about 2 bananas)

1½ cups whole wheat pastry flour

1 cup all-purpose flour, plus more for pan

2 teaspoons baking powder

½ teaspoon baking soda

½ teaspoon ground cinnamon

½ teaspoon salt

¼ teaspoon ground cloves

4 large eggs, separated

2 cups dark pure maple syrup, divided

3 tablespoons avocado oil or organic canola oil

2 tablespoons dark rum

1 teaspoon vanilla extract

1. Preheat oven to 350°F. Generously coat a 12-cup Bundt pan with nonstick cooking spray. Dust only the pan bottom with flour.

2. In a small bowl, combine pecans, maple sugar, and 2 tablespoons melted butter. Spread evenly around the pan. Arrange banana slices on top of maple sugar mixture.

3. In a medium bowl, whisk flours, baking powder, baking soda, cinnamon, salt, and cloves.

4. In a clean bowl, beat egg whites with clean electric beaters on medium speed for 2 to 3 minutes, until soft peaks form.

5. In a large bowl, beat egg yolks, mashed bananas, 1¼ cups syrup, oil, rum, and vanilla until smooth. Beat in remaining 4 tablespoons melted butter.

6. Stir flour mixture into wet mixture. Stir in one-third of the egg whites to lighten batter. Fold remaining egg whites into batter. Carefully pour batter on top of banana slices in pan. Bake for 48 to 55 minutes, until cake is puffed and springs back when lightly touched. Cool in the pan on a wire rack for 10 minutes. Run a knife along pan edge and then invert cake onto a cooling rack to cool completely.

7. Just before serving, in a medium saucepan fitted with a candy thermometer, bring remaining ¾ cup syrup to a boil over medium-high heat. Set up an ice bath next to the stove. Boil, without stirring, about 4 minutes, until syrup reaches 240°F. (Watch carefully so that syrup does not boil over.) Remove from heat and set the saucepan into the ice bath for 30 seconds to immediately stop cooking. The sugar mixture will thicken. Drizzle syrup over cooled cake.

Brown Butter Pudding Chômeurs

This humble sweet cake, born in Quebec during the Great Depression to serve to the unemployed, or *chômeurs*, is still popular in parts of Canada and New England. My version is made with a bit of coffee and brown butter.

Makes 8 servings | Active time: 10 minutes | Total time: 50 minutes

SAUCE

- 4 tablespoons unsalted butter
- ½ cup dark pure maple syrup
- 2 tablespoons strong coffee

CAKE

- ½ cup all-purpose flour
- ½ cup whole wheat pastry flour
- 2 teaspoons baking powder
- ½ teaspoon salt
- 2 eggs
- ⅓ cup nonfat or low-fat buttermilk
- ⅓ cup maple syrup
- 2 tablespoons avocado oil or organic canola oil
- 1 teaspoon vanilla extract

1. Preheat oven to 350°F. Place 8 4-ounce ovenproof ramekins on a baking sheet and lightly coat the insides with nonstick cooking spray.

2. In a small saucepan over medium heat, melt butter, swirling pan occasionally, 7 to 8 minutes, until melted and the milk solids are starting to brown. Remove from heat and carefully add syrup and coffee. Transfer sauce to a glass measuring cup or pitcher for pouring.

3. In a medium bowl, whisk flours, baking powder, and salt. Set aside.

4. In a medium bowl, whisk eggs, buttermilk, syrup, oil, and vanilla. Add flour mixture and stir. Transfer batter to a glass measuring cup or pitcher for pouring. Divide batter evenly among the prepared ramekins. Gently pour hot sauce over batter, dividing evenly.

5. Place the baking sheet of ramekins in the oven and bake for 18 to 22 minutes, until cakes are puffed and sauce is bubbling. Let cool for 30 minutes before serving.

Maple Carrot Cupcakes with Coconut Cream Cheese Frosting

I love these carrot cake cupcakes with coconut frosting, and my older daughter prefers them with Seven-Minute Maple Frosting (page 148). Either way, make sure you use the darkest available maple syrup so the maple flavor shines through.

Makes 12 cupcakes | Active time: 35 minutes | Total time: 3 hours

CUPCAKES

- ¾ cup white whole wheat flour
- ½ cup all-purpose flour
- 2 teaspoons baking powder
- 1½ teaspoons ground cinnamon
- ½ teaspoon baking soda
- ½ teaspoon salt
- ¼ teaspoon ground nutmeg
- 2 large eggs
- ¾ cup dark pure maple syrup
- ½ cup plus 1 tablespoon coconut oil, melted
- 1 tablespoon vanilla extract
- 1½ cups shredded carrots
- ½ cup raisins
- ½ cup finely chopped walnuts or pecans (optional)

FROSTING

- 1 15-ounce can full-fat coconut milk, refrigerated overnight (do not shake)
- 8 ounces cream cheese, room temperature
- ¼ cup dark maple syrup
- 3 tablespoons sweetened flaked coconut, toasted (optional)

1. Line 12 muffin tins with paper liners. Preheat oven to 375°F.

2. In a medium bowl, whisk flours, baking powder, cinnamon, baking soda, salt, and nutmeg. Set aside. In a large bowl, beat eggs and syrup with an electric mixer on medium speed until completely combined. Gradually beat in coconut oil and vanilla. Stir in carrots with a silicone spatula. Add flour mixture and stir to combine. Add raisins and walnuts (if using) and stir to combine.

3. Fill each tin well with about 1/4 cup batter. Bake for 16 to 18 minutes, until cupcakes are puffed and spring back when gently touched. A toothpick inserted into the center should come out with moist crumbs attached. Let cupcakes cool in the paper liners for about 10 minutes; remove from tin and cool completely on a wire rack.

4. Carefully open the can of coconut milk and scrape off top layer of solid fat. Place fat in a medium bowl and beat with an electric hand mixer on medium speed or a stand mixer on high speed, stopping once to scrape down the bowl sides, 60 to 90 seconds total, until light and fluffy.

5. Beat in cream cheese until smooth and creamy, about 1 minute, stopping once to scrape down the bowl sides. Gradually beat in syrup until smooth. Beat on high until fluffy, about 2 minutes.

6. Top each cupcake with frosting, sprinkle with coconut (if using), and serve.

Seven-Minute Maple Frosting

Use this frosting on Maple Carrot Cupcakes (page 146), or try spreading it over a gingerbread cake. It will also shine on a simple yellow cake.

Makes 6 cups | Active time: 15 minutes | Total time: 15 minutes

2 egg whites

1 cup dark maple syrup

¼ teaspoon white vinegar

½ teaspoon vanilla extract

Pinch salt

1. In a large saucepan or 8-cup double boiler, bring 1 to 2 inches of water to a boil. If using a saucepan, make sure a medium (8-cup) heatproof bowl will fit on top. Reduce heat to maintain a simmer.

2. Off heat, in the medium heatproof bowl or double boiler, beat egg whites, syrup, and vinegar with an electric hand mixer. Place the bowl over the simmering water and beat mixture for about 7 minutes, until glossy and fluffy; the egg whites should hold medium peaks. Adjust the heat under the double boiler if necessary to maintain a steady simmer. Remove bowl from heat and continue beating for 3 to 5 minutes, until mixture is cool. Beat in vanilla and salt. Frost as desired.

Maple Date Bread Pudding

When my husband and I got married, we had warm bread pudding instead of a traditional cake. I love the way the dates melt and bring out the maple's natural caramel notes. Try this dessert with Maple Yogurt Cream (page 165) or Maple Ice Cream (page 149).

Makes 12 servings | Active time: 20 minutes | Total time: 1 hour 40 minutes

1 cup dark pure maple syrup

¾ cup nonfat milk

½ cup half-and-half

6 large eggs

1 teaspoon vanilla extract

½ teaspoon salt

8 cups bread cubes, hearty firm white or multigrain, crusts removed

1 cup chopped, pitted soft dates

1 tablespoon turbinado sugar

1. Preheat oven to 325°F. Coat a 2-quart baking dish with nonstick cooking spray.

2. In a large bowl, whisk syrup, milk, half-and-half, eggs, vanilla, and salt. Add bread and dates and stir to combine, breaking up clumps of dates. Transfer to the baking dish, cover with foil, and bake for 45 to 50 minutes, until the center starts to puff. Remove foil and sprinkle the top with turbinado sugar. Increase heat to 350°F and continue baking for another 13 to 17 minutes, until the top is golden and crusty. Let cool for at least 20 minutes before serving.

Maple Ice Cream

I love this ice cream for many reasons. One is the pure maple flavor, which shines through. Another is that my culinary wheels rev to a fever pitch when I start dreaming up the potential pairings for desserts à la mode.

Makes 1 generous quart (8–9 servings) | Active time: 30 minutes | Total time: 4 hours

2 teaspoons unflavored gelatin

3 cups low-fat milk, divided

¼ cup heavy cream

6 egg yolks

1 cup dark pure maple syrup

¼ teaspoon salt

1. In a small dish, sprinkle gelatin over ¼ cup milk and allow to bloom. Set aside.

2. In a medium heavy-bottomed saucepan, heat remaining 2¾ cups milk and cream over medium-high heat until mixture is steaming hot. Remove from heat.

3. In a medium bowl, whisk yolks, syrup, and salt. Gradually pour in hot milk mixture, whisking constantly. Return mixture to the saucepan over medium-low heat, stirring with a wooden spoon, 7 to 8 minutes, until mixture thickens and coats the back of the spoon. You can tell it's ready by dipping a spoon and then running a finger across the mixture; if it leaves a clean line, the custard is thickened.

4. Remove the saucepan from heat and whisk in gelatin mixture until smooth. Pour custard through a fine-mesh sieve into a medium bowl. Set bowl into an ice bath to cool quickly, or transfer to refrigerator. Stir occasionally to speed cooling.

5. Add custard to an ice cream maker and process according to the manufacturer's instructions. Serve.

Maple Apple Almond Torte with Maple Cinnamon Glaze

A lot of baked goods, especially those with whole grains, grow slowly stale and unpalatable with time. But this torte is even moister and more delicious the day after it's baked. It's special enough to serve for a holiday table or humble enough to enjoy with a cup of coffee for breakfast.

Makes 10 servings | Active time: 25 minutes | Total time: 3 hours

TORTE

- 1 cup whole raw unsalted almonds
- 1 cup all-purpose flour
- ½ cup white whole wheat flour
- 1 teaspoon baking soda, sifted
- ½ teaspoon salt
- 2 large eggs
- 1 cup dark pure maple syrup
- 8 tablespoons unsalted butter, melted and cooled to room temperature
- 2 large yellow apples, such as Ginger Gold or Mutsu, peeled and diced

GLAZE

- 1 cup confectioners' sugar, sifted
- 3 tablespoons dark pure maple syrup
- 1 teaspoon apple cider vinegar
- ½ teaspoon ground cinnamon

1. Preheat oven to 350°F. Coat a 9-inch springform pan with nonstick cooking spray.

2. In a food processor fitted with a steel blade attachment, process nuts for 20 to 30 seconds, until finely ground. Add flours, baking soda, and salt and pulse to combine.

3. In a large bowl, beat eggs and syrup until smooth. Gradually beat in butter. Stir in almond mixture followed by apples. Transfer to the prepared pan and bake for 44 to 48 minutes, until torte springs back when lightly touched and a toothpick inserted into the center comes out with moist crumbs attached. Cool on a wire rack completely.

5. Make glaze: In a small bowl, stir sugar, syrup, vinegar, and cinnamon.

6. Run a knife along the edge of the pan. Remove sides and spread glaze over torte. Slice and serve.

Maple Apple Crumb Pie

Using a blend of Macintosh apples, which cook down and become soft, and firmer, sweeter varieties (Pink Lady is a good choice here) gives this pie filling better texture and flavor.

Makes 10 slices | Active time: 45 minutes | Total time: 5 hours

CRUST

- 1 cup whole wheat pastry flour
- ½ cup all-purpose flour, plus a bit more
- 1 tablespoon maple sugar or brown sugar
- ¼ teaspoon salt
- 4 tablespoons cold unsalted butter
- 2 tablespoons avocado oil or organic canola oil
- 3 to 5 tablespoons ice water

FILLING

- 1¼ pounds Macintosh apples, peeled and cut into thick slices (6 small apples)
- ¾ pound firm, sweet apples, peeled, cored, and cut into thin slices (2 medium apples)
- ¾ cup dark pure maple syrup
- 3 tablespoons all-purpose flour
- 2 tablespoons lemon juice
- 1 teaspoon ground cinnamon
- 1 teaspoon cornstarch

TOPPING

- ½ cup chopped walnuts
- ⅓ cup all-purpose flour
- ¼ cup old-fashioned oats
- 2 tablespoons unsalted butter, melted
- 2 tablespoons dark maple syrup
- Pinch salt

1. Make crust: In a food processor fitted with steel blade attachment, pulse flours, maple sugar, and salt until combined. Cut in butter and process until mixture resembles coarse meal. Remove lid and drizzle in oil. Replace lid and pulse 3 or 4 times. Remove lid and drizzle in 3 tablespoons ice water evenly around mixture. Pulse several times until mixture is even. Remove lid and squeeze mixture. If dough holds together but isn't tacky, form it into a ball. If it's crumbly and doesn't come together, drizzle another 1 to 2 tablespoons ice water and process quickly. Gather dough and flatten into a disk. Wrap in plastic wrap and refrigerate for at least 1 hour.

2. Place a rack in the bottom third of the oven. Preheat oven to 375°F.

3. Roll out dough on a lightly floured surface to a circle about 14 inches in diameter. Transfer to a 9-inch pie plate (not deep dish). Roll overhanging dough under itself all along the edges. Gently press dough into a short wall along the rim of plate and then crimp the edges. Set aside in a refrigerator.

4. Make filling: In a large bowl, stir apples, ¾ cup syrup, flour, lemon juice, cinnamon, and cornstarch.

5. Make topping: In a medium bowl, stir walnuts, flour, oats, butter, syrup, and salt. Work together with clean hands until mixture is evenly moistened and clumps together.

6. Add apple mixture to dough shell. Top evenly with crumb topping. Bake for about 30 minutes, until starting to brown. Reduce heat to 325°F and continue baking for 60 to 70 minutes, until filling bubbles. Let cool to room temperature before slicing, about 1½ hours.

Cranberry, Clementine, and Maple Clafoutis

Don't be surprised when this far-from-traditional clafoutis threatens to puff out of its pan. It won't, and it'll quickly fall back into place as it cools. Traditionally, clafoutis is served topped with powdered sugar, but I can't bring myself to cover up the jewel-like cranberries.

Makes 8 servings | Active time: 15 minutes | Total time: 1 hour 15 minutes

About 1 tablespoon unsalted butter, softened

3 large eggs

1 cup dark maple syrup

¾ cup nonfat milk

½ cup flour

2 tablespoons unsalted butter, melted

1 tablespoon clementine zest

1 teaspoon vanilla extract

1 cup fresh cranberries

2 clementines, segmented

1. Preheat oven to 350°F. Grease a 9-inch deep-dish pie plate with butter.

2. In a blender, puree eggs, syrup, milk, flour, butter, zest, and extract for about 15 seconds, until smooth.

3. Pour batter into the prepared pie dish. Scatter cranberries on batter. Arrange clementine segments over top. Bake for 38 to 45 minutes, until clafoutis is puffed and cranberries have burst. Serve warm.

Maple Bourbon Pumpkin Pie

Bourbon is one of those ingredients that pulls the essence of maple out of a recipe and highlights it. And you only need a few teaspoons to do it.

Makes 10 servings | Active time: 35 minutes | Total time: 3 hours

CRUST

- 1 cup whole wheat pastry flour
- ½ cup all-purpose flour, plus more for dusting
- 1 tablespoon maple sugar or brown sugar
- ¼ teaspoon salt
- 4 tablespoons cold unsalted butter, cut into chunks
- 2 tablespoons avocado oil or organic canola oil
- 3 to 5 tablespoons ice water

FILLING

- 1 14-ounce can pure pumpkin puree
- 1 cup dark pure maple syrup
- ⅔ cup sour cream
- 3 large eggs
- 4 teaspoons bourbon
- 2 teaspoons pumpkin pie spice

1. In a food processor fitted with steel blade attachment, pulse flours, maple sugar, and salt until combined. Add butter and process until mixture resembles coarse meal. Remove lid and drizzle in oil. Replace lid and pulse 3 or 4 times. Open lid and drizzle 3 tablespoons ice water, spreading drops evenly around mixture. Process until mixture just comes together. If it doesn't, drizzle another 1 to 2 tablespoons ice water and process until dough forms a mass. Flatten into a disk, wrap dough in plastic wrap, and refrigerate for at least 1 hour to firm up.

2. Place a rack in the lower third of the oven. Preheat oven to 375°F.

3. Roll out dough on a lightly floured surface. Transfer to a shallow 9-inch pie plate. Roll overhanging dough under itself along the edges. Gently press dough into a short wall along the rim of plate and then crimp the edges. Chill dough while you prepare the filling.

4. In a large bowl, whisk pumpkin puree, syrup, sour cream, eggs, bourbon, and pumpkin pie spice.

5. Pour filling into the dough shell and bake for about 20 minutes, until crust starts to brown. Reduce heat to 325°F and continue baking for another 35 to 45 minutes, until filling starts to puff along the outside and the center barely jiggles. Let cool completely before serving, about 1½ hours.

Rustic Pear Galette

Don't let the word galette scare you off; think of this vanilla bean–flecked dessert as a pie without the pie plate. To make the pastry flakier, this recipe uses a technique called fraisage. Again, this is not as scary as it sounds—it's just the French culinary term for smearing butter into the dough to create sheets of fat inside.

Makes 6 servings | Active time: 25 minutes | Total time: 2 hours

¾ cup plus 2 tablespoons all-purpose flour, divided, plus more for dusting

½ cup white whole wheat flour

½ cup plus 2 tablespoons maple sugar, divided

½ teaspoon salt

4 tablespoons unsalted butter, cut into small chunks

3 to 5 tablespoons ice water

Seeds from 1 vanilla bean

1 tablespoon freshly squeezed lemon juice

3 ripe pears, peeled, cored, and cut into wedges

1 egg white, lightly beaten

1. In a medium bowl, whisk 3/4 cup all-purpose flour, white whole wheat flour, 1 tablespoon maple sugar, and salt. Add butter and toss with flour to coat. Quickly rub butter and flour together by hand, leaving some pea-sized chunks. Add just enough water to moisten and toss with a fork to combine. Work with hands to bring together flour mixture as a dough, adding water if necessary. Transfer to a lightly floured surface. Work in butter chunks by smearing dough away from you on the work surface 3 to 5 times. Shape dough into a disk, wrap in plastic wrap, and refrigerate for 40 minutes.

2. Preheat oven to 350°F. Line a large rimmed baking sheet with parchment paper.

3. In a large bowl, gently stir vanilla bean seeds, juice, remaining 2 tablespoons flour, and ½ cup maple sugar. Gently stir in pears and set aside. Mixture will become more liquid as it sits.

4. Lightly dust work surface with flour. Roll out dough to a 12- to 14-inch-wide circle. Transfer to the prepared baking sheet, letting dough drape over the edges. Arrange pears in a circular pattern in the center, leaving a 2½- to 3-inch border. Scrape maple mixture from the bowl and drizzle over fruit. Fold dough edges over fruit, leaving the center uncovered. Brush egg white over top. Sprinkle remaining 1 tablespoon maple sugar over top. Bake for 40 to 50 minutes, until crust is golden and filling is bubbling. Let cool before cutting.

Maple Lemon Squares

If you share these with others—and I don't blame you if you want to keep them all to yourself—you will surely get many requests for this recipe!

Makes 16 2-inch squares | Active time: 25 minutes | Total time: 2½ hours

¾ cup white whole wheat flour

½ cup plus 2 teaspoons all-purpose flour, divided

2 tablespoons maple sugar

2 tablespoons avocado oil or organic canola oil

2 tablespoons unsalted butter, melted

6 eggs, divided

1 teaspoon water

½ teaspoon salt

1 cup dark pure maple syrup

1 tablespoon lemon zest

½ cup freshly squeezed lemon juice (2–3 lemons)

1. Preheat oven to 350°F. Coat an 8-inch-square glass or ceramic baking dish with nonstick cooking spray.

2. In a food processor fitted with a steel blade attachment, pulse whole wheat flour, ½ cup all-purpose flour, and maple sugar. Drizzle oil and butter over flour mixture and process to combine. Scrape the bowl sides with a spatula.

3. In a small dish, beat 1 egg, water, and salt until foamy. With the food processor running, drizzle egg through the feed tube. Mixture will be very crumbly—do not overprocess. Transfer to the prepared baking dish and press mixture into the bottom and slightly up the sides. Prick all over with a fork and transfer to the oven. Bake for about 20 minutes, until crust is set but not browned.

4. Meanwhile, in a large bowl, whisk remaining 5 eggs until whites and yolks are well combined. Whisk in syrup, zest, and juice to combine. When crust comes out of the oven, use a pastry brush to immediately brush remaining 2 teaspoons flour into the fork holes and cracks in the crust. Quickly pour lemon mixture over crust. Do not worry if it looks like the filling runs under the crust.

5. Carefully return pan to the oven. Reduce oven temperature to 325°F and bake for 20 to 23 minutes, until filling no longer is liquid when the pan is jiggled. Let cool completely, about 1½ hours. Slice into 16 squares. For firmer texture, refrigerate, covered, for 4 hours or overnight before slicing.

Maple Bacon Peanut Brittle

A word to the wise: this brittle is addictive, so you may have to hide it from yourself if you have any intention of sharing or giving it away.

Makes 1 pound | Active time: 35 minutes | Total time: 1 hour 35 minutes

2 teaspoons baking soda

¼ teaspoon salt

1¾ cups golden or amber maple syrup

¼ cup golden syrup or light corn syrup

2 tablespoons butter

5 strips bacon, cooked to crispy and finely crumbled (about ½ cup)

1 cup unsalted peeled peanuts, toasted

1. Line a rimmed baking sheet with a Silpat or coat generously with nonstick cooking spray. Spray a heatproof silicone spatula with nonstick cooking spray. Stir baking soda and salt in a small dish and set aside.

2. In a large heavy saucepan, bring syrups to a boil over medium-high heat, stirring occasionally. Fit saucepan with a candy thermometer and cook until mixture reaches the hard-crack stage, or 300°F. Remove from heat and stir in butter. Sprinkle in baking soda and salt mixture and stir to fully incorporate; the mixture will bubble and foam. Stir in bacon and peanuts.

3. Pour onto the baking sheet and spread with the prepared spatula. Let cool ¼ hour to 1 hour before cutting or breaking into pieces.

Salted Maple Penuche Fudge

Spoiler alert: this is my new signature holiday gift. Candy making used to kind of freak me out, but once I got over my fear, I fell madly in love. Don't be afraid to try it. Just make sure you read through the whole recipe first.

Makes 1½ pounds | Active time: 45 minutes | Total time: 4 hours

2 cups golden pure maple syrup

⅓ cup packed brown sugar

⅓ cup heavy cream

2 tablespoons golden cane syrup or light corn syrup

1 teaspoon table salt

1 cup chopped toasted nuts, such as walnuts, pecans, or hazelnuts

½ teaspoon salt flakes, such as Maldon

1. In a 3- to 4-quart heavy-bottomed saucepan, bring syrup, sugar, cream, cane syrup, and table salt to a boil over high heat, stirring often, until sugar is melted. Insert a candy thermometer into the boiling mixture and adjust heat so that flames are not licking the sides of the pan. Or on an electric stove, turn down heat just far enough that the heating element heats only the bottom of the pan.

2. Dip a pastry brush into water and brush the saucepan sides to transfer any sugar crystals into the syrup. Boil, undisturbed, 5 to 7 minutes, until mixture reaches the soft-ball stage at about 244°F (see "The Soft-Ball Test" for tips). Remove from heat and immediately pour into a clean, dry mixing bowl to stop the temperature from rising. Allow to cool without stirring for 30 to 40 minutes, until mixture reaches 120°F.

Note: you may have to tilt the bowl to get the bulb of the thermometer deep enough to give an accurate temperature reading.

3. Coat an 8-inch-square baking dish with nonstick cooking spray.

4. Beat maple mixture with a handheld electric mixer on medium to high speed, incorporating as much air as possible. Increase beater speed as mixture thickens, rotating the bowl, tilting it, and lifting the beaters to cool and aerate mixture quickly, 10 to 15 minutes. The mixture will suddenly become opaque and less shiny, and it will stiffen considerably. Working quickly, stir in nuts, scrape mixture into the prepared baking dish, and flatten it with a spatula or damp, clean hands. Sprinkle salt flakes over top. Refrigerate for about 2 hours, cooling completely, before cutting into pieces.

How to Do the Soft-Ball Test

Maple syrup is a natural ingredient, with varying properties from batch to batch, and temperature, altitude, and cooking equipment all affect the results. So you'll need to do a soft-ball test. The mixture does not form a true ball but is more of a sticky mat at the bottom of the glass. To test, dip a clean, dry spoon into the boiling maple mixture and drizzle it into a glass of ice-cold water. If it the mixture dissolves in the water, continue heating. Start checking the mixture when it reaches 238°F. This particular ratio of ingredients attains the soft-ball stage at 240°F to 244°F. Note that on humid or rainy days, you may have to cook it to an even higher temperature.

Pure Maple Candy

Making pure maple candies can be a true art form that takes lots of trial and error. Don't worry: even if you miss the window of opportunity for the right texture, and the mass solidifies before it's molded, you can just melt it down again. You'll need maple candy molds, so check the Resources for supplies (page 170).

Makes 58 small candies | Active time: 30 minutes | Total time: 30 minutes

3 cups golden pure maple syrup
  Tiny pinch unsalted butter

1. Place syrup in a tall-sided 3½- to 4-quart heavy-bottomed saucepan. Dot butter about 1½ inches from the top edge of the saucepan rim. (This will keep the syrup from boiling over.) Fix a candy thermometer to the side of the saucepan so that the sensor does not touch the bottom of the pot.

2. Set timer for 15 minutes and bring syrup to a boil over medium-high heat. Make sure the flames from a gas stove do not lick the sides of the saucepan. Do not stir. Watch carefully when the temperature reaches 232°F, about 15 minutes from the time the syrup goes over the heat.

3. Cook until the temperature reaches 242°F (or 32°F above water's boiling point.) Let sit off the heat for about 2 minutes, until the bubbles subside completely and the temperature drops to 238°F.

4. Immediately pour into a 4-cup heatproof glass measuring cup and stir with a clean metal spoon for 30 seconds to 2 minutes, until you can feel a slight grain on the bottom of the measuring cup. It will feel like undissolved sugar in the bottom of a hot drink.

5. Quickly pour syrup into molds. Allow to cool undisturbed for 2 hours, until completely set. Turn candies onto parchment or wax paper. Store at room temperature in a dry place for 4 days. Freeze for longer storage (which will also make the candies more creamy.)

Maple Yogurt Cream

This lightly sweet alternative to whipped cream acts as a cool, creamy foil to so many desserts. To make it sweeter, substitute 3 tablespoons maple sugar for the maple syrup.

Makes 2½ cups | Active time: 5 minutes | Total time: 5 minutes

¾ cup nonfat plain Greek yogurt
2 tablespoons dark pure maple syrup
　Pinch salt
¾ cup whipping cream

1. In a large bowl, whisk yogurt, syrup, and salt until smooth. In another clean bowl, whisk cream or beat with an electric mixer on medium-high speed until medium peaks form. Fold whipped cream into yogurt mixture. Serve.

Maple Pear Ginger Sorbet

This sorbet *(shown left)* has just the right level of ginger to tickle the palate without overpowering the maple. If you like a stronger ginger flavor, add more to taste. Try scooping it into tall glasses and pouring cream soda on top for a twist on a soda float.

Makes 8½-cup servings | Active time: 30 minutes | Total time: 3 hours

4 ripe pears, peeled, cored, and chopped
1 cup dark maple syrup
1 teaspoon finely grated ginger, or more
　to taste

1. In a medium heavy-bottomed saucepan over medium-high heat, bring pears and 1 cup water to a simmer. Reduce heat to medium-low and simmer for 7 to 12 minutes, until pears are tender. Transfer mixture to a blender, add syrup and ginger, and carefully puree until smooth. Chill in a metal bowl set over another bowl of ice water, stirring often. Alternatively, refrigerate until cold.

2. Process pear mixture in an ice cream maker according to the manufacturer's instructions. Transfer to a quart-sized storage container, freeze until firm, and serve.

Resources

Gathered here are explanations of techniques and ingredients,
as well as sugaring and culinary resources for cooking with maple.

Knife Skills

So what's the difference between a mince and a dice? Here's a guide to some of the knife skills called for in Maple's recipes.

Dice: Dicing means cutting something into cubes. It's more precise than chopping. A small dice means ¼-inch cubes, a medium dice means ½-inch cubes, and a large dice means 1-inch cubes. A tiny dice—¹⁄₁₆-inch cubes—is called a brunoise. Mincing something is like making a tiny brunoise—teeny cubes. For these recipes, the dice is a medium (½-inch) cube, unless otherwise specified.

Chop: Chopping means cutting something in a more haphazard fashion. Chopping is appropriate when it's fine if the pieces cook less evenly. If a soup will be pureed, for example, chopping is clearly quicker and easier than dicing into perfect cubes. I like to call for chunks sometimes, too. That means you don't even need to make a cube. Just work with the natural curvature of the vegetable or whatever you're chunking up.

Julienne: This cut is sometimes called matchstick because of its shape. The result is roughly ⅛ by ⅛ by 2 inches long. This cut is nice if a more formal presentation is important. A mandoline is a quick way to achieve this cut.

Pantry Notes

These are some of the ingredients featured in the recipes throughout this book, along with a brief explanation of why I choose them.

Avocado Oil: Avocado oil has a high smoke point and a neutral flavor. I use it interchangeably with organic canola oil. See Canola Oil.

Broth: Note that "reduced sodium" is not the same as "low sodium." Regular chicken broth has about 860 mg of sodium per cup. Reduced-sodium broth is around 570 mg and will not always be called that on the label. Low sodium is under 100 mg per cup.

Butter: Use unsalted butter unless otherwise specified.

Buttermilk Powder: Dehydrated buttermilk is available in the baking aisle of large supermarkets. It has to be refrigerated after you open it, but it lasts much longer than fresh liquid buttermilk. I use it as a concentrated ingredient in dressings and dips to add intense buttermilk flavor without extra liquid.

Canola Oil: I love canola oil because it has no taste and contains the good amounts of heart-healthy monounsaturated fats and alpha-linolenic acid. Because the majority of canola oil is genetically modified, I recommend looking for organic so that you know for certain that it is not. If you prefer, use avocado oil.

Chia Seeds: This ingredient is gaining popularity as a healthy plant-based source of essential fatty acids and fiber. Try adding them to smoothies or sprinkling them on salads.

Coconut Milk: Available in both light and regular (full fat), this product is sugar free. It can be found in the Asian section of large supermarkets. Shake the can before opening; otherwise, the liquid and fat will be separated.

Coconut Oil: Solid at room temperature, this plant-based oil is mostly saturated. It adds a pleasant coconut flavor to baked goods and can be used on the stovetop as well. Find it in jars with other cooking oils in natural food stores and large supermarkets. To melt coconut oil, heat in 30-second burts in the microwave or over low heat on the stovetop.

Eggs: All the recipes in *Maple* call for large eggs.

Flax Seed Oil: Keep this highly volatile oil in the refrigerator. It is high in Omega-3 fatty acids. Anything more than a subtle fishy flavor means that it has gone bad.

Maple Cream: Also called maple butter, this creamy spread is unparalleled on a warm toasted English muffin. It is available commercially, or, if you need a good arm workout, you can make it at home. It is made from pure maple syrup cooked to 234°F, cooled, and beaten until creamy. Store it in the refrigerator.

Maple Sugar: Maple sugar is pure maple syrup that has had all the water removed through heating. It is heated to 260°F to 265°F (hard-ball stage) and then stirred constantly and rapidly as it cools.

Powdered Egg Whites: A shelf stable product that is made from pasteurized and dehydrated egg whites, this is a safe way to add egg white to a recipe that may not be cooked to safe temperatures. It can be reconstituted and used just like regular egg whites in many recipes such as meringues.

Quinoa: Find it with the grains in supermarkets or at the health food store. Some brands are rinsed and some aren't. If the package doesn't specify, it's a good idea to rinse the quinoa under cool water in a fine-mesh sieve before cooking to remove its soaplike coating. Naturally gluten free, it gives a great plant-based boost of fiber and protein.

Salt: In these recipes, assume that salt is iodized table salt, unless otherwise specified.
- **Kosher Salt:** A coarser salt. Unfortunately, you cannot just substitute kosher salt for iodized one-to-one. Kosher has about half the sodium, and the exact amount varies by brand. Look at the nutrition label and compare the amount of sodium to determine the ratio.
- **Salt Flakes:** Sometimes called Celtic Sea Salt Flakes, this salt has large crystals that add a nice crunch to a dish.

Toasted Nuts: To toast nuts, bake them on a baking sheet in a 350°F oven for 6 to 10 minutes, until lightly browned and fragrant.

Toasted Coconut: To toast shredded or flaked coconut, bake it on a baking sheet in a 350°F oven for 2 to 4 minutes, until golden brown.

Turbinado Sugar: Also marketed as raw sugar, this sugar is made from cane juice that has not been fully refined to white granulated sugar. It is light brown, its larger crystals make a crunchy topping for desserts.

White Whole Wheat Flour: This flour is milled from a variety of wheat known as hard white winter wheat. It is lighter in color than whole wheat flour, mild in flavor, and has a protein level of 13%. If you can't find it, substitute whole wheat flour. As with all whole grain flours, storing it in the freezer will keep the natural oils from going rancid.

Whole Wheat Pastry Flour: This finely milled whole grain flour is made from soft wheat, which means it contains less protein than whole wheat flour, so it makes for more tender baked goods. It can be found in the baking aisle of large supermarkets or at the health food store. Store long-term in the freezer.

Resources

King Arthur Flour Store

www.kingarthurflour.com

This is the best source for unusual ingredients and baking equipment that I have found. It is employee owned and operated in Vermont. Many of the ingredients used in this book, including white whole wheat flour, whole wheat pastry flour, gluten-free all-purpose flour, vanilla beans, and maple sugar, are available through its website and mail order catalogue. It also offers an excellent selection of kitchen tools and equipment, including rasp-style graters, baking sheets, parchment paper, and cheesecloth.

Leader Evaporator

www.leaderevaporator.com

Candy molds and other candy-making supplies, bottles, and sugaring equipment.

Tap My Trees

tapmytrees.com

Fantastic resource for getting your backyard sugaring operation off the ground. Offers detailed information on getting started as well as equipment you'll need.

Cornell Sugar Maple Research and Extension Program

If you ever want to delve further into the science behind maple and sugar making, this website is a bounty of information. It's also a great place to go if you have questions about sugar science and candy making.

maple.dnr.cornell.edu

Regional and State Sugar Makers Associations

You'll find chapters in all U.S. sugar making states as well as Canada. These associations are wonderful resources for all maple-related information. Whether you're interested in setting up your own sugaring operation or just want to visit an operational sugar house, start here.

Slopeside Syrup

www.slopesidesyrup.com

This small family-run sugaring operation is in my town in Vermont. It's owned and operated by four cousins on the mountainside where their family runs a ski area. They make consistently great syrup, and they're some of the friendliest guys around.

Goodrich Maple Farm

www.goodrichmaplefarm.com

You can go right in to this sugarhouse in Cabot, Vermont, and watch owner Glen Goodrich and his huge locomotive-sized evaporator at work. Also offers seminars for budding sugar makers and maple cooking classes.

Silloway Maple

www.sillowaymaple.com

In addition to fantastic syrup, this smaller operation in Randolph Center, Vermont, sells maple cream and granulated sugar through its website.

Sweet Hearts of Vermont

aobrien@gmavt.net

Pure maple candy makers who specialize in wedding and event favors.

Metric Conversions

Use these rounded equivalents to convert between the traditional American systems used to measure volume and weight and the metric system.

volume

American	Imperial	Metric
¼ tsp		1.25 ml
½ tsp		2.5 ml
1 tsp		5 ml
½ tbsp (1½ tsp)		7.5 ml
1 tbsp (3 tsp)		15 ml
¼ cup (4 tbsp)	2 fl oz	60 ml
⅓ cup (5 tbsp)	2? fl oz	75 ml
½ cup (8 tbsp)	4 fl oz	125 ml
⅔ cup (10 tbsp)	5 fl oz	150 ml
¾ cup (12 tbsp)	6 fl oz	175 ml
1 cup (16 tbsp)	8 fl oz	250 ml
1¼ cups	10 fl oz	300 ml
1½ cups	12 fl oz	350 ml
1 pint (2 cups)	16 fl oz	500 ml
2½ cups	20 fl oz (1 pint)	625 ml
5 cups	40 fl oz (1 qt)	1.25 L

oven temperatures

	°F	°C	Gas Mark
Very cool	250–275	130–140	½ –2
Cool	300	148	2
Warm	325	163	3
Medium	350	177	4
Medium hot	375–400	190–204	5–6
Hot	425	218	7
Very hot	450–475	232–245	8–9

weights

American/British	Metric
¼ oz	7 g
½ oz	15 g
1 oz	30 g
2 oz	55 g
3 oz	85 g
4 oz (¼ lb)	110 g
5 oz	140 g
6 oz	170 g
7 oz	200 g

American/British	Metric
8 oz (½ lb)	225 g
9 oz	250 g
10 oz	280 g
11 oz	310 g
12 oz (¾ lb)	340 g
13 oz	370 g
14 oz	400 g
15 oz	425 g
16 oz (1 lb)	450 g

Index

Index

Acknowledgments

"When we try to pick out anything by itself, we find it hitched to everything else in the Universe."
—John Muir

Taking on the topic of Pure Maple Syrup is no small feat, especially for a flatlander. When I started this project, I wondered how I could do justice to the subject that Vermonters know so much about and that is so deeply embedded in North Country history and culture. I wondered how I could honor the traditional maple recipes that have been perfected over generations while still creating something new and fresh.

I am so grateful that I pushed aside my fear. Not only did I fall head over heels in love with maple syrup, I got to know the generosity of the maple community. I was incredibly happy to hear so many people's stories and about their love of maple syrup and what it means to them. Thank you all so much for your generosity, for your support, and for giving me the courage to make this idea a reality.

I give deepest thanks to:

The maple sugar makers who bring us the best sweetener on the planet. Their hard work and dedication to their craft humble me.

Jack Linn, who was the first person I called when I considered taking on the subject of maple syrup. My deliveries of cookies are not enough to repay him for his help.

My agent, Samantha Marsh, who helped me turn my idea into a well-crafted plan that became the seeds of this book. And to Lisa Ekus, who so kindly waited for my idea to crystalize. To Hinda Miller, who coached me to just go for it. To Molly Stevens for being my cookbook author mentor, and for helping me choose which path in the yellow wood to travel upon.

My editor Tiffany Hill, who believed in this project and allowed my vision to become a reality. Her patience, attention to detail, and unfailing kindness have made this process a joy. Designer Alison Oliver, who made these pages shine. I love the fact that I could completely trust that her vision would be better than what I could imagine.

My testers! I still cannot thank them enough. Christine Burns Rudalevige and Sarah Strauss, for their meticulous test reports and troubleshooting and fixing. And my faithful volunteer cross-testers, Marcy, Diane, Kristina, Heather, Rachael, Jen, Peggy, Neil, Lori, Lori, Lori, Kay, Liz, Amy, and Mom. I thank them so much for showing enthusiasm for these recipes, finding all those typos and mistakes, and testing until we got it just right. And mostly for their honesty when things just weren't good. I love it when mistakes are made in the testing process!

Ellen Falsgraf, for allowing me to hit the ground running. And Liz Neily, for food and prop styling relief. They were like a breath of fresh air that I so desperately needed!

My network of blogging friends who lifted me up and carried my blog with beautiful guest posts while my mind was steeping in maple syrup. And to my dear readers of Healthy Seasonal Recipes, they are the wind in my sails every day. I mean that!

Matt Gordon of the Vermont Sugar Makers Association, for walking me through the basics and getting me excited about the growth of the maple syrup industry. Sam and Emma Marvin, for their perspective and for allowing me to have faith that this new view of cooking with maple was a story that needed to be told. Roger Brown of Slopeside Syrup, for helping me organize my gray matter.

My daughters, for eating strange combinations of multiple maple-spiked recipes all cobbled together for dinner (again!), and for letting Mommy work through our afternoons together. Thank you for being my front line of taste testers, and for being patient while I was occupied with all matters maple.

Lastly, my husband, Jason. Without him, I would have never caught the maple bug, and for that I am eternally grateful. Not just for putting up with the overfull fridge, the sticky cabinet knobs, and the sinkfuls of dishes. For the unyielding support he gave me through this project, and for never doubting my choice to put the book high on my list of priorities. I wouldn't be here without him.